DEVELOPED BY THE ROYAL YACHTING ASSOCIATION

Know Your Boat's Diesel Engine

D1561301

AN ILLUSTRATED GUIDE TO MAINTENANCE, TROUBLESHOOTING, AND REPAIR

Andrew Simpson

International Marine / McGraw-Hill
Camden, Maine · New York · Chicago · San Francisco
Lisbon · London · Madrid · Mexico City · Milan · New Delhi
San Juan · Seoul · Singapore · Sydney · Toronto

The McGraw·Hill Companies

1 2 3 4 5 6 7 8 9   RRD SHEN   0 9 8

© 2006, 2008 Royal Yachting Association.

First published in the United Kingdom 2006 as the *RYA Diesel Engine Handbook* by The Royal Yachting Association.

Library of Congress Cataloging-in-Publication Data
Simpson, Andrew, 1940–
     Know your boat's diesel engine : an illustrated guide to maintenance, troubleshooting, and repair / Andrew Simpson.
          p.   cm.
     Originally published: RYA diesel engine handbook / by the Royal Yachting Association, 2006.
     Includes index.
     ISBN-13: 978-0-07-149343-7 (pbk. : alk. paper)
   1. Marine diesel motors—Handbooks, manuals, etc. I. Title.
     VM770.S53 2007
     623.87'236—dc22   2007024457

ISBN 978-0-07-149343-7
MHID 0-07-149343-3

Questions regarding the content of this book should be addressed to

International Marine
P.O. Box 220
Camden, ME 04843
www.internationalmarine.com

Questions regarding the ordering of this book should be addressed to

The McGraw-Hill Companies
Customer Service Department
P.O. Box 547
Blacklick, OH 43004

Retail customers: 1-800-262-4729
Bookstores: 1-800-722-4726

Illustrator: Sarah Selman.
Edited for North America by Bob Armstrong.

Contents

Introduction

THE DIESEL ENGINE GETS ITS NAME from its inventor, Rudolf Diesel, who was born in Paris in 1858 of Bavarian immigrant parents. He studied at Munich Polytechnic and after graduating worked as a refrigeration engineer. However, his real interest lay in engines. In August 1893, his prototype pressure-ignited model ran for the first time. It later exploded, nearly killing him. It was not until 1897 that he built a really successful engine. This was the first sure step in a process of development that continues to this day.

Although the principles remain the same, the modern diesel engine has become more refined. It's lighter, quieter, and more powerful for its weight than anyone could have imagined even a few years ago. Where inboard marine engines are concerned, it has become almost the only choice for sailing yachts and workboats and the preferred option for many recreational powerboats—particularly the larger ones.

The inherent simplicity of diesel engines makes them very reliable, but like all machinery they are certainly not infallible. Since many aspects of seamanship have to do with reducing risk and knowing how to act when the unexpected happens, it should come as no surprise to learn that the same applies to diesel engines. A wise skipper will maintain his engine properly—thereby ensuring it will give the best possible service—and will make sure he knows exactly where to turn if it develops problems. Incidentally, the words "his" and "he" are used only to keep the text as simple and uncongested as possible. They could just as easily be "her" and "she," since this subject is by no means an exclusively masculine domain.

The objects of this book are to provide a sound understanding of how diesel engines and their various ancillaries work and to give basic guidance on maintenance and troubleshooting procedures. Used in conjunction with your own engine manufacturer's manual, there is little else you should need to know.

How Diesel Engines Work

U NLIKE GASOLINE ENGINES, WHICH EMPLOY an electrical spark to initiate combustion, diesel engines rely on "pressure-ignition," a phrase that describes the principle well. When air is compressed rapidly it becomes extremely hot. Once it reaches about 400°C (752°F) it's hot enough to ignite a suitable fuel injected into it. This temperature is reached when the air is compressed to about a fourteenth of its original volume—and an engine capable of achieving this would be said to have a "compression ratio" of 14:1. In practice, higher compression ratios are used to provide a comfortable margin—the range 18:1 to 20:1 being common. This compares to about 10:1 for gasoline engines and explains why diesels must be more solidly constructed to cope with the higher loads.

Those two commodities, air and fuel, are all diesel engines need to run. Yes, battery power is almost invariably employed to crank and start them, but—with certain exceptions—once started they will operate without electricity. The exceptions include electrically governed engines and those with solenoid fuel shut-offs or common rail injection—all subjects we will deal with later. Figures 1.1 through 1.6 illustrate various types of diesel engines.

So, in order to function, a diesel engine must gather together a quantity of air, compress it quickly so that it heats, then introduce some fuel that will combust and expand.

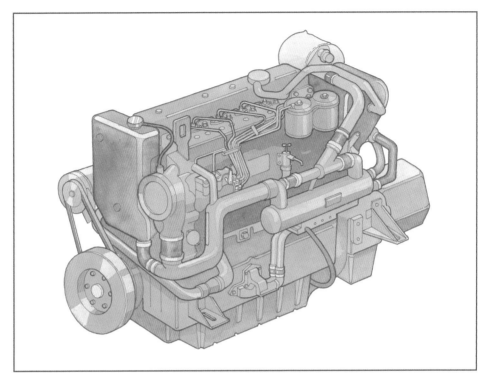

Figure 1.1   A large six-cylinder engine—the type you might find in a powerboat.

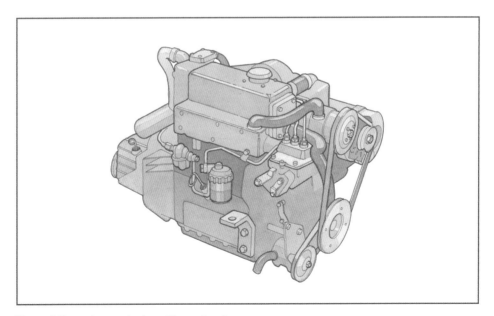

Figure 1.2   A three-cylinder sailboat diesel.

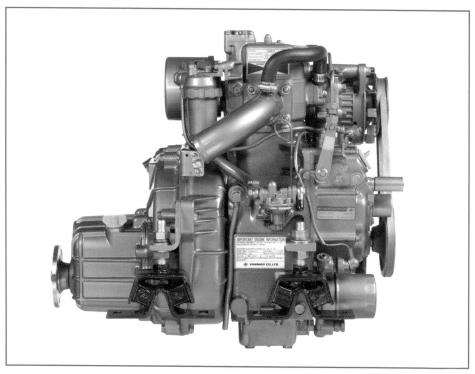

Figure 1.3   A one-cylinder, 9-hp sailboat auxiliary. (Courtesy Yanmar)

Figure 1.4   A three-cylinder sailboat auxiliary. (Courtesy Volvo Penta)

Figure 1.5   A six-cylinder engine—the type you might find (in pairs) in mid-sized powerboats. (Courtesy Cummins MerCruiser)

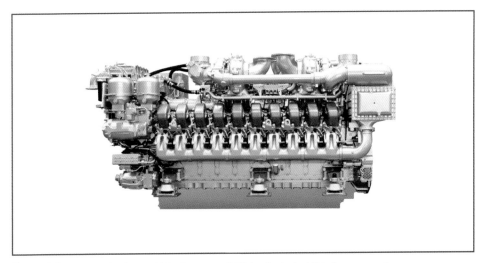

Figure 1.6   A 20-cylinder, 5766-hp "monster." We've included this for comparison purposes only; it is much larger than you'd find on any vessel that doesn't have a full-time crew, including an engineer. (Courtesy MTU Detroit Diesel)

THE FOUR-STROKE CYCLE

The inventor of the four-stroke cycle was Nicholas August Otto who died in Cologne, Germany, about the time Rudolf Diesel was presenting his first engines. Occasionally, you may still hear the sequence described as the "Otto cycle," though most of us are more familiar with the term "four-stroke cycle." They are, of course, the same thing. This cycle is sometimes expressed as "suck, squeeze, bang, and blow"—inelegant but to the point (Figure 1.7). Each of the strokes relates to the actions of a piston within a cylinder and of a pair of valves controlling the intake and exhaust paths for air and the spent gases that result from combustion. The timing of the various actions must be precisely coordinated. The four strokes are as follows:

1. **The induction or intake stroke.** This is the "suck" part of the sequence. The piston withdraws down the cylinder and draws in air from outside through the open intake valve. The exhaust valve is closed.
2. **The compression stroke.** Now the piston is moving back up into the cylinder. Both the intake and exhaust valves are closed. Having no escape, the air is compressed and gets hotter and hotter. Just a little before the piston reaches the top of the stroke, atomized diesel fuel is sprayed into the cylinder at high pressure and . . .
3. **The expansion or power stroke.** . . . Bang! The fuel and air mixture in the cylinder ignites and burns—essentially a contained explosion. The expanding gases drive the piston down the cylinder with great force, which, once converted to rotary energy by the crankshaft, serves to turn the propeller.

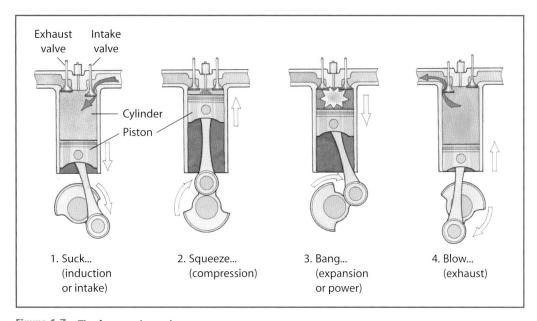

Exhaust valve   Intake valve

Cylinder
Piston

1. Suck...
(induction
or intake)

2. Squeeze...
(compression)

3. Bang...
(expansion
or power)

4. Blow...
(exhaust)

Figure 1.7   The four-stroke cycle.

4. **The exhaust stroke.** The exhaust valve opens and the piston pushes back up the cylinder to expel all the spent gases. Once it reaches the top, the exhaust valve closes and the intake valve opens. The cycle is ready to start again.

TURBOCHARGING

Engines that suck air into their cylinders solely by the action of their induction strokes are described as "naturally aspirated." In a perfect world, the air sucked in by each cylinder would be equal to its volume. By this we mean the volume of the cylinder above the piston at the bottom of its stroke—aptly called the "swept volume." In reality, friction and other influences make it somewhat less. But let's ignore this for now and assume that when we refer to an engine of one liter (about 61 cubic inches) capacity, we're talking about an engine that should theoretically draw in one liter (61 cubic inches) of air during the course of one complete cycle of all its cylinders—for example, 500cc (30.5 in.^{3}) each for a two-cylinder engine.

Now, since there's an optimum mix ratio between air and fuel, it follows that the more air you can draw in, the more fuel can be mixed with it and the greater will be the release of energy when that mixture combusts. Given this simple relationship, it's easy to understand why the outputs of naturally aspirated engines are directly related to their capacity. In other words, the larger they are, the more powerful they will be. Fortunately, there's a device that can fool an engine into believing that it's bigger than it actually is. It's called a turbocharger (Figures 1.8 through 1.10).

A turbocharger forces air into the cylinder, compressing it and making it denser. Now, holding a greater quantity of air than a naturally aspirated cylinder, extra fuel can be added without upsetting that ideal mix ratio. Once combusted, the result will be a much more powerful expansion stroke.

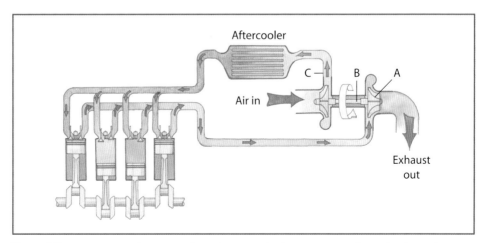

Figure 1.8   How a turbocharger works. Only multicylinder engines can be turbocharged because the exhaust flow must be continuous.

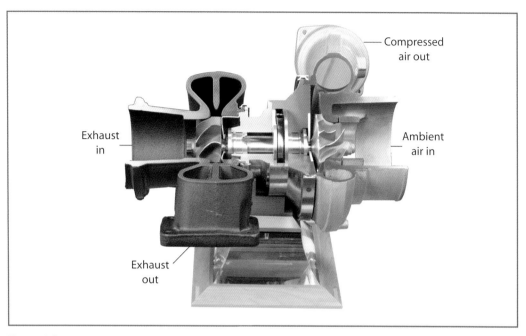

Compressed
air out

Exhaust
in

Ambient
air in

Exhaust
out

Figure 1.9   Cutaway view of a turbocharger. (Courtesy NASA's John H. Glenn Research Center)

Figure 1.10   Superchargers are more effective at low revs.

Of course, nothing is gained without cost. Since the turbocharger is driven by a turbine in the exhaust flow, some energy is lost in the greater resistance experienced on the exhaust stroke. However, this is more than compensated for by saving the energy lost in natural aspiration, in which the induction stroke must laboriously drag the air in from outside, unassisted.

A supercharger does the same job, but is powered differently—usually by a belt or shaft. Some large engines have both turbochargers and superchargers. The supercharger boosts the power at low revs, with the turbocharger taking over when it's turning fast enough to be effective.

A turbocharger works as follows (see Figures 1.8 and 1.11):

A. Hot exhaust gases spin a turbine positioned in their flow. Having done their work, the gases are then turned 90° toward the exhaust elbow, where they're cooled in the usual way by injected seawater. Incidentally, since the

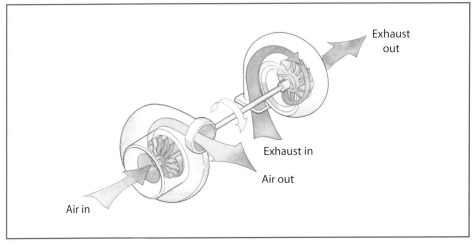

Figure 1.11   How a turbo works.

exhaust flow must be continuous, only multicylindered engines can be turbocharged.

B. The turbine is connected directly by the shaft to the compressor and, of course, spins at the same speed—as much as 120,000 rpm! It draws in the air through the air filter and . . .

C. . . . sends it on under pressure to the inlet manifold, from where it passes into the cylinders.

AFTERCOOLING OR INTERCOOLING?

There's a further trick that will wring even more power out of the engine. Cold air is denser than warm air, so anything you can do to cool it down will reduce its volume and allow more of it to be admitted to the cylinders. The words "aftercooling" and "intercooling" mean exactly the same thing and—as if that weren't confusing enough—so does the phrase "charge-air cooling." They all describe a straightforward process in which the air from the turbocharger, unhelpfully warmed by being compressed, is passed through a seawater-cooled "heat exchanger" to cool it down again (Figure 1.12). The way heat exchangers work is explored more in Chapter 4.

The combination of turbocharging and intercooling can greatly boost an engine's output. For example a well-known four-cylinder sailboat auxiliary puts out 55hp in its naturally aspirated form, rising to 75hp when turbocharged and a lusty 100hp with an intercooler added. Of course, the internal stresses on bearings and other components mount with every horsepower gained. In the interests of reliability, manufacturers have learned to make compromises between what's possible and what's practical.

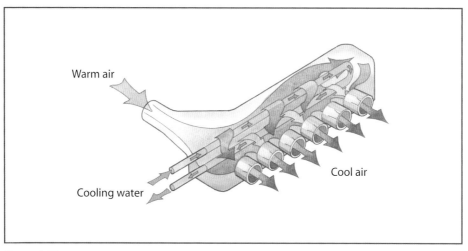

Warm air

Cool air

Cooling water

Figure 1.12 Intercooling.

THE TWO-STROKE CYCLE

Two-stroke diesels are relatively rare beasts—almost never seen as small sailboat auxiliaries and only rarely in recreational power craft. They are more usually seen in the largest sizes of engines, particularly the slow revving ones like those propelling merchant ships. In smaller sizes, the older Detroit Diesels (Series 53, 71, V-71, 92, and 149) are about the only remaining examples—and there are certainly enough of them still in service to deserve inclusion in this book.

The two-stroke Detroit Diesel 8V-71TA engines are no longer manufactured, but there were thousands of them installed in powerboats of all types and sizes over many, many years. Because of these numbers and the engines' inherent toughness, you'll still find a substantial number of them in service today (Figure 1.13).

Unlike four-stroke engines, whose cylinders only produce power on every fourth stroke, the two-stroke fires on every other stroke. Because they fire twice as often, two-strokes are more powerful than four-strokes for any given size. And since they have no intake valves, they are also mechanically less complex. This might seem to be an irresistible combination until we learn that their emissions are higher and they're less fuel efficient.

Let's look at the two-stroke cycle (Figure 1.14).

1. **Piston at bottom dead center (BDC).** The sequence is best described beginning when the piston is at the bottom of its stroke. A mechanical blower forces air into the cylinder through the intake ports. This both compresses the air and drives the spent gases out through the open exhaust valve at the top. Although it isn't absolutely essential that two-stroke diesels be supercharged, this is almost always the case.

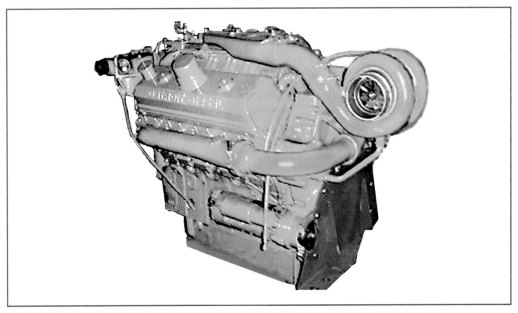

Figure 1.13   Two-stroke Detroit Diesel 8V-71TA. (Courtesy MTU Detroit Diesel)

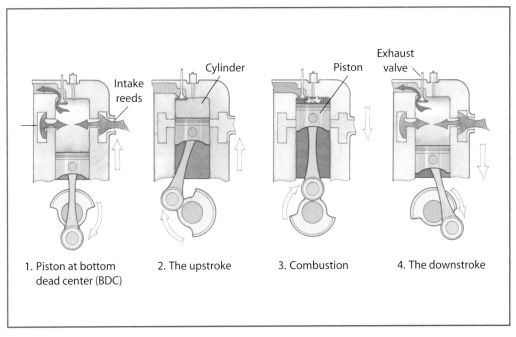

Figure 1.14   Two-stroke cycle.

2. **The upstroke.** Almost as soon as it moves upward, the piston covers and seals the intake ports. The exhaust valve closes and there's no way for the air to escape. The heat of the compressed air rises as its volume is reduced.
3. **Combustion.** Just before the piston reaches the top of its stroke, atomized fuel is sprayed into the cylinder and ignites, driving the piston down again.
4. **The downstroke.** Once the piston drops below the level of the inlet ports, the exhaust valve also opens and allows the new inrush of air to purge the spent gases as before. This sequence is repeated for every turn of the crankshaft.

DIRECT AND INDIRECT INJECTION

So far we've looked at diesels in which the fuel is injected into the top of the cylinder—"direct injection," in the vernacular. There's another method, which makes use of a small recess in the cylinder head known as a precombustion chamber, or simply a "prechamber." The fuel is injected into this prechamber where it combusts. The rapidly burning gases then propagate into the cylinder itself, forcing the piston downward.

Indirectly injected engines (Figure 1.15) are a bit quieter than direct injection, and for this reason have gained ground in the automotive world. Unfortunately, they're less easy to start, so they often need a helping hand before they fire. This help takes the form of "glow plugs"—electric heater elements that prewarm each precombustion chamber for a few seconds before cranking. If your engine has glow plugs (and, most probably, a concomitant "preheat" switch), you can be sure

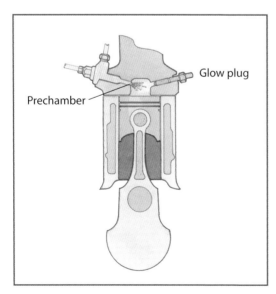

Figure 1.15   Indirect injection.

that it's indirectly injected. In Figure 1.16, compare the cross section of an indirectly injected cylinder head (1.16a) with the directly injected cylinder head (1.16b).

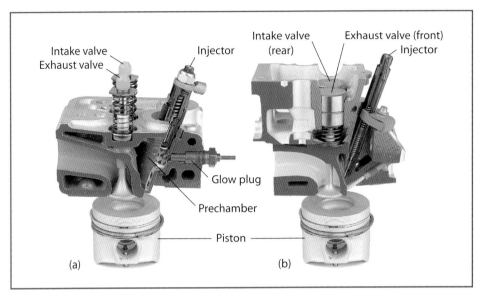

Figure 1.16   Indirect (a) and direct (b) injected cutaways. (Courtesy Technolab SA; www.technolab.org)

CHAPTER 2

The Fuel System

ALTHOUGH TODAY'S ENGINES CONSUME FUEL derived from mineral oil, this was not always the case. Rudolf Diesel experimented with pulverized coal dust—of which there was plenty in the Ruhr valley where he worked—and, at the 1900 World's Fair in Paris, his engines were powered by peanut oil. Later, in 1937, a movement to produce diesel fuel extracted from industrial hemp was scuppered by petroleum-friendly interests in the U.S. Congress who cynically—and entirely wrongly—sought to demonize the scheme by linking it with marijuana! It's interesting to reflect that hemp and other suitable vegetables form a resource the world may again have to turn to at some future date. Indeed, there is currently a considerably renewed interest in the so-called "biodiesel" fuels, principally those derived from corn and soybean oil.

WHAT IS DIESEL FUEL?

Diesel fuel is basically a distillate of crude oil to which various other ingredients are added. We don't need to know much about its chemistry, but you may occasionally hear mention of a "cetane number," which is applied to diesel in much the same way as "octane" is to gasoline. But the comparison isn't identical. Their scales are actually inverse. This means that a high-octane fuel will have a low cetane number and vice versa.

Cetane is a hydrocarbon that is easily ignited by compression. By assigning it a rating of 100, it can be used as a benchmark against which the ignition quality of another fuel can be compared. For example, the cetane numbers of the standard grade diesel fuel we buy at the pumps will range between 40 and 45, with the higher number having the better ignition quality. Producers often vary the precise composition to suit local and seasonal conditions. Although the name on the pump might be the same, a fuel sold in the tropics will have a lower cetane number than one formulated for harsh winters. Remember that the variations have no bearing on overall quality. There's nothing to be gained by searching for fuels with higher cetane numbers, since the number just tells us how easily the fuel will ignite when compressed, not how much power it will release.

THE BASIC FUEL SYSTEM

A typical diesel fuel system (Figure 2.1) forms a circuit around which the fuel passes in an endless parade. Fuel starts from the tank, where it is stored, and is then drawn through a pre-filter by the lift pump. From there it goes through yet another (finer) filter before reaching the injection pump. The pump helps itself to however much the engine wants and sends it on to each of the injectors in turn. The surplus fuel goes back to the tank via the return pipe to join the parade again. Incidentally, the fuel should always return to the tank from whence it came. To return it to another tank could cause that tank to overflow.

The lift pump, fine filter, injection pump and injectors are all parts of the engine. The tank, shut-off valve, pre-filter, and most of the fuel lines are supplied and fitted by the boatbuilder.

Let's look at them one at a time.

THE TANK

A fuel tank is one of those fit-and-forget items few of us even bother to think about—yet it's here that many of our troubles begin. Diesel tanks can be made from a wide variety of materials: mild steel, stainless steel, aluminum, fiberglass-

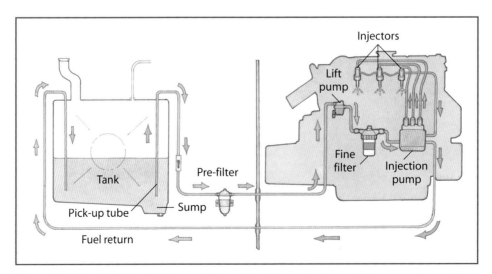

Figure 2.1   A typical diesel fuel system. The engine draws what it needs from a continuously circulating flow.

reinforced plastic (known as either FRP or GRP), molded or welded polyethylene, or nitrile rubber impregnated fabrics—the last, of course, being flexible. Each of these has its virtues and vices.

Perhaps the most potentially treacherous is mild steel. A tank might appear sound from the outside but could be severely rusted within. The rust is caused by water condensation, and there's some debate as to how this arises. Many would argue that it's simply a result of the temperature changes that occur between day and night. As the fuel level drops, moist air is pulled in through the vent. A minority opinion claims that there can never be enough water vapor inside a tank—not even a nearly empty one—to have a significant effect. This last group would point the accusing finger toward water-contaminated fuel—either tainted at its source or later through the air vent or a leaking filler cap.

All of which makes for fascinating discussion but is of little consolation to the boatowner. The fact is that mild steel tanks can and do rust internally, and the detritus thus formed can very quickly block the pre-filter. But rust isn't the only threat.

DIESEL "BUGS"

Microbiological contamination of the fuel can pose a serious problem. A variety of organisms—including bacteria, yeasts, fungi, and algae—will thrive in the mix of water and fuel that lies at the bottom of many tanks. The organisms arrive either in contaminated fuel or as airborne spores, entering through vents and filler hoses. As they grow, die, and biodegrade the fuel, they form a slimy black, brown, or green sludge that can quickly plug the filters and bring the whole system to a standstill. The sludge is very corrosive, capable of doing serious damage to components it contacts.

This is a major headache. Biocides will kill the little varmints, but their corpses remain unless physically removed. Since they need both fuel and water to survive, the best protection is to make sure there's little or no moisture in the tank. Some experts recommend routinely dosing the fuel with a biocidal additive as a preventive measure. Others believe you should wait until action is needed.

THE IDEAL TANK

Most of us live with the tanks the boatbuilder supplied. The only time we're offered a choice in the matter follows the failure of the original—a minor disaster as the mess can be appalling. However, it can provide a welcome opportunity to improve the installation.

The first question is what materials to use. Stainless steel tanks are resistant to rusting but are almost invariably fabricated from thin gauge stock that can flex and fatigue—usually cracking at the welds. Aluminum tanks are subject to oxidization pitting, which can eventually lead to leaking. Flexible tanks, on the other hand, will handle any amount of flexure but are notoriously susceptible to abrasion. Fabricated or molded plastic tanks are immune from corrosion and are becoming increasingly popular, but must be stoutly made to be really reliable.

Although it isn't always possible to arrange, ideally all fuel tanks should have a drainage sump at their lowest point. Since water is heavier than diesel fuel, it will sink to the bottom and collect in the sump. It should then be a relatively simple task to open the drain cock and draw off any water lying there (Figure 2.2a). An alternative is to have an accessible inspection hatch through which a pump can be inserted (Figure 2.2b). Either way, as soon as pure, clean diesel fuel starts to emerge, you will know you have removed a significant threat. Also, look out for sediment, which might warn of the existence of bugs. A sample from the depths will tell you a lot about the health of your fuel system.

Another valuable feature is the dip (or pick-up) tube type outlet. By drawing the fuel from a short distance above the bottom of the tank, you minimize the risk of including water and heavy sediment with it. Of course, this means that you effectively reduce your tank's capacity, but it's never sensible to run the dregs through your system anyway.

Thin-walled tanks should be well baffled and given plenty of support, not just along their bases but also along the sides. The loads imposed by fuel sloshing around inside can be considerable. Try to limit flexing as much as possible.

Shut-off valves should be located outside the engine compartment where they can be closed in the event of a fire. And, since they are prime suspects in water contamination incidents, tank vents should be positioned where they're unlikely to be swamped. All fuel lines should be fire resistant. Fuel hoses must meet specifications set by both the American Boat & Yacht Council (ABYC) and the U.S. Coast Guard; the designations are stamped on the line. Don't use anything less than U.S. Coast Guard Type A1 or Society of Automotive Engineers (SAE) J1527, and secure hoses against chafe.

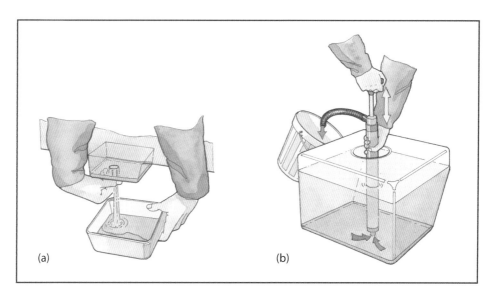

(a)   (b)

Figure 2.2   A sump and drain tap (a) are the easiest way to remove contaminants from your tank . . . but you can also use a hand pump (b) poked down through an inspection hatch.

Figure 2.3 Approved fuel hose. (Courtesy Trident Marine Systems)

Approved fuel hose is more complex than it appears from the outside. But the outside will always show the approval numbers, in this case that it meets (or exceeds) the standards for USCG type A1 (Figure 2.3).

Metal tubing should be seamless copper or cupro-nickel (preferred) with a minimum wall thickness of 0.027 inch. Joints in lines need to be air tight and kept to a minimum. Ideally, the only breaks in seamless continuity will be at the tank, at the shut-off and/or tank-selection manifold valves, at the pre-filter, and at the engine. Always use hose for the final connection to the engine because vibration will work-harden metal tubing and make it brittle. Because simply clamping hose over metal tubing will invite trouble (even well-clamped hoses can slide off and/or leak), be sure to use proper barbed end fittings and all-stainless steel hose clamps.

WATER-SEPARATING FILTER (PRE-FILTER)

The first defense against contaminated fuel is to be careful where you buy it. The second is your pre-filter—commonly called the primary filter—most types of which will also strip water from the fuel.

A typical example is shown in Figure 2.4. The fuel enters through the inlet (A) and is sent downward into a bowl (B). There, an arrangement of fixed vanes causes the fuel to rotate, creating a centrifugal effect that separates water particles and heavy sediment and deposits them in the bottom of the bowl. The fuel then rises inside the casing and passes through a filter element (C) before being sent on to the engine.

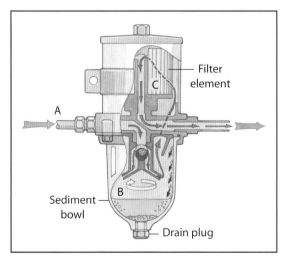

Figure 2.4 The pre-filter, often called the primary filter, is indeed the primary line of defense against contaminated fuel.

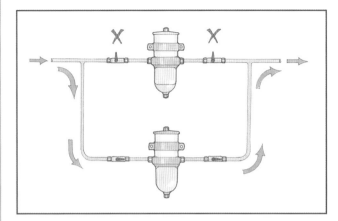

Figure 2.5   Bypass filters.

The bowl may either be of glass, metal, or plastic. Transparent bowls allow you to see if any contaminants have been collected, in which case they can be drained off through the drain plug. Opaque bowls need draining periodically, just in case. U.S. Coast Guard regulations require that glass- or plastic-bowled filters be either situated outside the engine space or be fitted with a metal heatproof shield, which inevitably partially obscures them from view. (For severe service, it is recommended that an all-metal bowl be used.) Some filters have a pair of electrodes that, when immersed in collected water, will complete an electrical connection to sound a warning alarm.

Bypass Filters

An excellent precaution is to have a pair of filters fitted in parallel (Figure 2.5). If one becomes blocked, the other can be brought into service immediately without losing propulsion. If this seems like overkill, it's worth remembering that an immaculate system can be seriously compromised by just a single intake of contaminated fuel. The risks of this happening might be negligible in regions where standards are high, but they increase mightily once you stray into less salubrious waters.

Having two filters allows you to run an engine on one while changing the replaceable element in the other (Figure 2.6). Note the vacuum gauge. It can help you know when it's time to change elements by showing diminished efficiency in the lift pump caused by filter restriction. When you are drawing five pounds of vacuum, it's time to change elements.

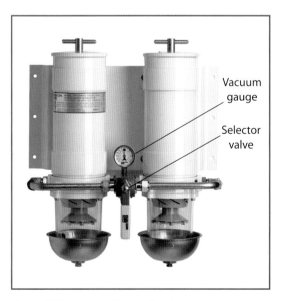

Vacuum gauge

Selector valve

Figure 2.6   A pair of Racor filter/water separators.

To reiterate, bypass filters allow you to clear one filter while running the engine on the other. You might have to repeat the task several times, but at least it presents the chance of getting home. Incidentally, the selector valve also effectively isolates the "off-line" filter, which limits the air that can enter the system when changing filter elements.

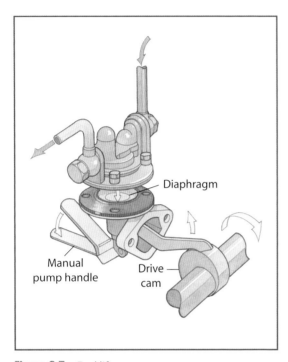

Figure 2.7 Fuel lift pump.

FUEL LIFT PUMP

The role of these relatively simple devices is to deliver fuel to the injection pump. Actually, they deliver an excess of fuel. Injection pumps will take only a little of what's offered, using what remains to lubricate and cool their mechanisms before sending it back along the return pipe to the tank. Since the amount they deliver isn't critical, lift pumps can afford to keep plenty on hand to offset unhelpful influences such as resistance caused by partially clogged filters or the suction head arising from tanks mounted low.

The most common type of lift pump is driven directly by the engine, and often has a small external handle so it can be operated manually for bleeding air from the system (Figure 2.7). Although there was a time when they could be stripped and serviced, modern ones are often throwaway units supplied complete. However, there's no cause for concern here. Lift pumps are both reliable and long-lived. It's not unusual for them to complete thousands of hours of service.

FINE FILTER (SECONDARY FILTER)

In cleanliness terms, this is the last chance. Beyond this point the fuel goes on to the most expensive single item on the whole engine—the injection pump—where even the tiniest particle of grit can cause grievous damage.

Filters are categorized by the size of the particles they allow through. The customary unit used to define particle size is the micron—one millionth of a meter or 0.00004 inch. Not very large, I'm sure you will agree. And, whereas a typical prefilter might fall into the 10 to 50 microns range, the fine filter (Figure 2.8) is more stringent at 2 to 10 microns.

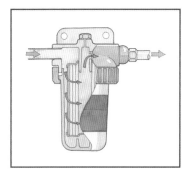

Figure 2.8   Fine filter—commonly known as the secondary filter.

At this point we should sing a short paean of praise in favor of two-stage filter systems. Diesel fuels contain tarry particles called "asphaltenes." Being small, soft, and pliant, they present no serious threat to the fuel injection process, but they tend to stick to the fibers of the first filter element they encounter. If this is the pre-filter, the fine filter lying downstream will be left relatively unsullied, and is therefore better able to remove what remains.

Incidentally, no matter how clean your fuel may appear, the ever-present asphaltenes will continue to clog up your filters. There couldn't be a better reason for changing them regularly.

THE INJECTION PROCESS

The role of injection pumps is crucial to the proper working of diesel engines. Why this should be so is easily understood, since they perform an extremely demanding job. After receiving the fuel from the lift pump they must deliver precisely metered quantities of fuel to each injector, exactly on time and at very high pressure—and they must do so over and over again (Figure 2.9).

In case there's any doubt as to what's involved, let's put it in perspective. A fraction of a second before the end of every compression stroke, a minute quantity of fuel (typically about 0.00002 liter—which is just 20 millionths of a liter or *four thousandths of a teaspoon!*) must be injected into the cylinder with a timing accurate to within 60 millionths of a second. The duration of each injection must be precisely controlled, and every cylinder must receive exactly the same amount of fuel at the same point in its cycle.

Such is the precision of these mechanical marvels that only skilled specialists should venture inside. And, since entry is denied to our DIY fumblings, it's not essential that we know exactly how they work. But it's certainly helpful to have a general idea. All injection pumps use plungers to both create the pressure and push the fuel along the delivery pipes to the injectors. There are three ways of achieving this: two are mechanical and the third is electrical, with variations on each theme.

The first types are known as "inline" pumps. These have a plunger for every cylinder, with each plunger operating once for every turn of the crankshaft. Then there are "distributor" (or "rotary") pumps, which have a single plunger and a mechanism to direct the fuel to each cylinder in turn. On a four-cylinder engine, for instance, the plunger will operate four times for every revolution. Finally, there are electromechanical injection pumps that use solenoids to actuate their plungers. Needless to say, these are controlled by computers, which can vary both the timing and the amount of fuel delivered. Mechanical pumps are timed by direct gearing to the engine, and variations in fuel quantity are usually achieved by adjusting the amount that is allowed to "spill" back into the return system.

The injection pump includes the throttle control. However, this word is borrowed from gasoline engines and is technically incorrect. Gasoline engines tradi-

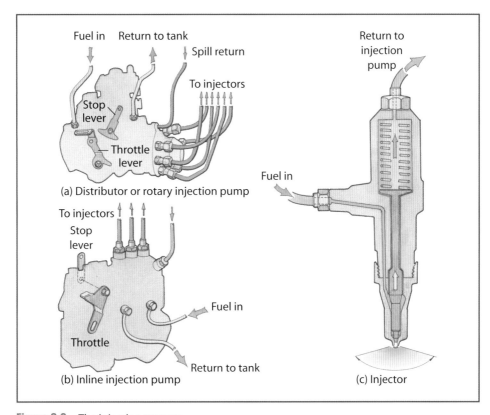

Fuel in   Return to tank
Spill return
To injectors
Stop lever
Throttle lever

(a) Distributor or rotary injection pump

To injectors
Stop lever

Throttle

(b) Inline injection pump

Fuel in

Return to tank

Return to injection pump

Fuel in

(c) Injector

Figure 2.9   The injection process.

tionally had carburetors whose air intakes were "throttled" to increase or decrease the amount of fuel/air mixture allowed to enter the cylinders. By contrast, a diesel engine doesn't throttle its air intake. Instead it varies the amount of fuel entering the cylinder—which already contains air—thereby altering the fuel/air ratio. Put another way: gasoline engines run on a constant fuel/air ratio, while diesel engines always have more air than is needed.

It's one of the main reasons why diesels are more fuel efficient.

TODAY'S FUEL-INJECTED GASOLINE ENGINES, which are also more fuel-efficient than the old carbureted variety, inject the fuel along with the air (which is still often "throttled" to control the amount of fuel/air mixture entering the cylinders) on the induction stroke, with a spark providing ignition at the end of the compression stroke. Diesels intake air only and then inject the fuel after compression has raised the air temperature sufficiently to allow ignition.

Connected internally to the throttle control is a governor—usually a simple centrifugal device—that helps maintain constant boat speed in varying conditions. If, for example, you meet a headwind, the engine will come under increased load and slow down. The governor senses the drop in revs and tweaks the throttle to release more power.

On some engines—notably two-stroke Detroit Diesels—the plunger action is incorporated in the injector unit itself, one entire unit being required for each cylinder. These can be operated either mechanically or electronically, and eliminate the need for conventional injection pumps and the high-pressure fuel lines that accompany them.

COMMON RAIL SYSTEMS

Fast gaining ground on road vehicle engines, this relatively new technology is now making a significant appearance on marine diesels, too. Common rail engines burn cleaner, quieter, and are generally more fuel efficient than conventional types (Figure 2.10). The downside is that they are electronically dependent, though the computer that controls injection can also be used to troubleshoot engine problems and often, even warn of impending abnormalities before they become serious problems. Either of these benefits can give electronic dependence somewhat of an upside, as well.

A common rail injection system raises the fuel to a very high pressure and stores it in a central accumulator tube—the "common rail" from which it gets its name. From there it is delivered to electronically controlled injectors, which introduce it to each cylinder in turn as a very fine mist, often in a number of extremely rapid spurts, further increasing efficiency.

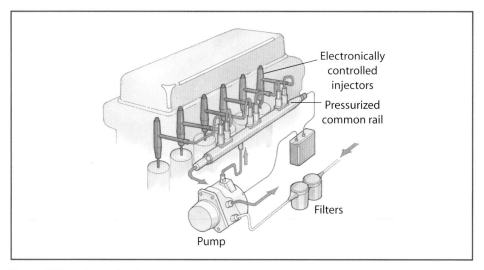

Figure 2.10   Although efficient, common rail systems are totally reliant on electronics.

CHAPTER 3

The Air System

AS WE COVERED IN THE FIRST FEW PAGES of this book, air is the second essential ingredient in the combustion process that drives all diesel engines. To starve an engine of air is as bad as starving it of fuel, and makes no sense at all since it costs us nothing to be generous.

It's not always understood how much air an engine needs (Figure 3.1). A four-stroke diesel engine is basically an air pump to which a combustion cycle has been added. It might be thought that a naturally aspirated engine of, say, one liter (61 cubic inches) capacity would draw in one liter (61 cubic inches) of air with each revolution—that is to say that at 3,000 rpm it would consume 3,000 liters (which is three cubic meters or nearly four cubic yards) every minute. Despite the best efforts of engineers to minimize the effects, restrictions in the intake flow make this impossible.

Figure 3.1   It's easy to underestimate the amount of air a large engine needs.

How efficiently a diesel takes in air is defined by its "volumetric efficiency": the proportion between its swept volume and what it actually aspirates, expressed as a percentage. With a volumetric efficiency of 80%, our one liter (61 cubic inches) engine would take in 2,400 liters (3.1 cubic yards) of air, which is still a huge amount. Turbocharged engines are much greedier. A large diesel running at cruising revs can easily consume a volume of air equal to a fair-sized room every single minute.

Unfortunately, while we appreciate what our engines do for us, their appearance, noise, and oily smell are less welcome. There's a tendency, therefore, to entomb them in insulated compartments deep in our boats—tastefully hidden from our tender susceptibilities but not in situations in which they will prosper. It's beyond the scope of this book to describe how every engine space might be ventilated. Suffice it to say that if we want our engines to serve us well, it's vital that we allow them to breathe.

AIR FILTERS

Whereas land-based engines must cope with all sorts of airborne debris, marine diesels live in relatively dust-free conditions. But that doesn't mean we want them to inhale small abrasive objects that might damage their mechanisms.

The defense against this is yet another filter (Figure 3.2).

Diesel engine air filters are made variously of mesh, foam, paper, and cotton wadding. Some filter elements are disposable; others can be washed and used again and again. Check your engine manual to see what type you have.

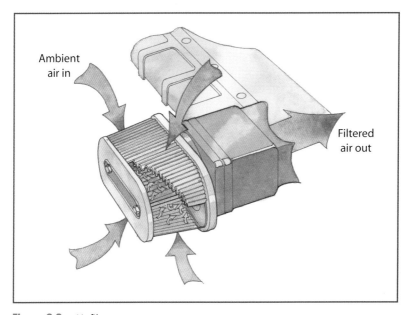

Ambient air in

Filtered air out

Figure 3.2   Air filter.

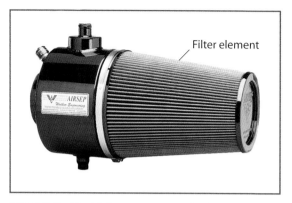

Filter element

Figure 3.3 The Walker Airsep not only filters incoming air, it also helps keep all of the lube oil within the engine. (Courtesy Walker Engineering)

Instead of using the engine maker's basic air filters, many builders now equip their boats with the Walker Airsep closed crankcase system (Figure 3.3). The Airsep not only assures clean air for the intakes, it also reduces crankcase pressure, which causes the engine to operate in a vacuum. The direct benefits include reduction or elimination of most seal leaks, less lube oil being forced by the rings into the cylinders, and reduction of oil being vented through the crankcase breathers (which also offers the indirect but valuable benefit of a cleaner engine compartment).

When the Airsep removes the lube oil from the blowby gases, the remaining water vapor and raw diesel fuel is re-inducted into the air intake system (Figure 3.4). On turbocharged and aftercooled engines, this helps prevent the build-up of grit on the turbocharger blades or the accumulation of oil residue in the aftercooler. Finally, the inducted water vapor reduces the temperature of combustion, which results in increased engine efficiency (as discussed in Chapter 1).

Airsep filters can be cleaned if you follow the manufacturer's instructions. Keep in mind, however, that this element not only filters the air, but also plays an

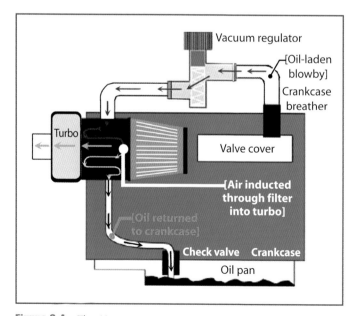

Figure 3.4 The Airsep process.

important role in the operation of the unit as a whole. So when it is time for replacement, the manufacturer recommends that you always use genuine Walker Airsep filter elements if your boat is equipped with this system.

EXHAUST

Having ushered in the air, mixed it with fuel and compressed it sufficiently to ignite it, the engine then has to get rid of the spent gases to make way for the next cycle. Since exhaust gases are both hot—about 450°C (842°F)—and generally unpleasant, they have to be handled with care. And there's a performance issue, too. Diesel engines are particularly susceptible to exhaust back pressure, so a poorly designed system can have many consequences, one of which is to sap power.

Figure 3.5 shows two typical arrangements: one with the engine's exhaust manifold above the waterline and the other with it below. On leaving the manifold (A) the gases pass on to the exhaust elbow or riser where, at the injection point (B), they meet the seawater hitherto used to cool the engine. If the engine is near or below the waterline, a siphon break, looped up above the waterline,

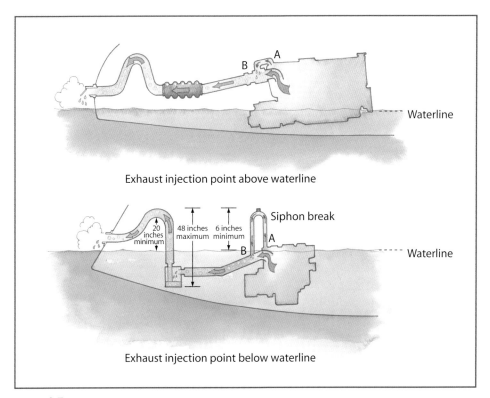

Exhaust injection point above waterline

Exhaust injection point below waterline

Figure 3.5   Two typical exhaust injection points.

must be added upstream of the injection point to ensure that water isn't drawn back into the engine.

The action of the water mixing with the exhaust gases cools them rapidly. It also reduces their volume and partially silences them. By now, the gas and water mix is cool enough to be handled by nonheatproof materials. The exhaust hose is usually spirally reinforced rubber, and the watertrap can be of FRP (fiberglass) or plastic. Note that the security of these components is entirely dependent on that crucial flow of water.

If uncooled exhaust gases were to flow through them they would melt or scorch, possibly releasing harmful chemicals into the cabin. Incidentally, because diesel fuel is combusted with an excess of oxygen, there's very little deadly carbon monoxide in their exhaust emissions—a fact that still wouldn't encourage you to breathe the stuff, of course.

WARNING

Even if the cooling waterflow is only temporarily interrupted, check the exhaust for damage.

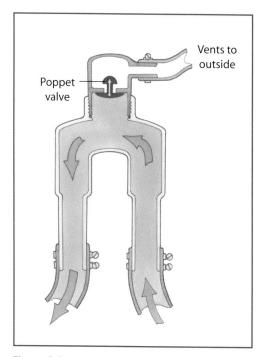

Figure 3.6   Siphon break.

Poppet valve

Vents to outside

SIPHON BREAKS

These are simply loops of hose introduced into the raw-water system and taken up above the waterline. On an indirectly cooled engine the loop is usually between the pump and the heat exchanger inlet or (as shown in Figure 3.5) between the heat exchanger outlet and the exhaust elbow injection point. On raw-water-cooled engines, the loop can be between the pump and the engine block inlet or between the thermostat and the exhaust injection point. In both cases, if the loop is in the hot part of the system, heat-resistant hose must be used.

To break the siphon, at the highest point in the loop you will find either a one-way valve or a small-bore vent tube led outside, often into the cockpit (Figure 3.6). These should be at least 150 mm (6 inches) above the static waterline and, on sailing yachts, as central as possible to minimize the effects of heeling.

Care must be taken to keep the valves (or vent tubes) free of salt crystals. If the vents become blocked, the siphons remain intact and any protection from flooding is removed.

WATERTRAP SILENCERS

These serve two functions. They reduce noise by about a further 50% and also provide a reservoir in which to collect the water present in the hose when the engine stops. While in operation, the contents of the exhaust are made up of about 85% gas and 15% water, so the watertrap must have a capacity of at least 15% of the volume of those parts of the hose that will drain into it.

A lift-type watertrap (Figure 3.7) also acts as a silencer, or muffler. It must have enough capacity to contain the water running back into it.

As we touched on earlier, watertraps can be of plastic (Figure 3.8) or FRP. To these must be added stainless steel. Both the plastic and FRP types are immune from corrosion but could be seriously damaged if the exhaust runs dry—particularly the plastic ones, which will fail in a matter of seconds. On the other hand, stainless steel watertraps are well able to bear the heat but their welds tend to corrode. It's all a matter of choice.

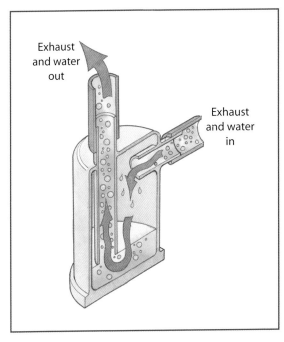

Figure 3.7   A lift-type watertrap.

Figure 3.8   A plastic watertrap.

EXHAUST TEMPERATURE ALARMS

Considering the possibly dire consequences of an exhaust failure, it pays to take precautions. Exhaust alarms are easy to fit and fairly inexpensive. The sensors on some must be introduced into the exhaust flow, usually through the wall of the hose (Figure 3.9); others clamp on externally.

Figure 3.9   Typical exhaust alarm system. A sensor is introduced into the exhaust flow, usually through the wall of the hose, and triggers an alarm if the temperature becomes excessive.

Exhaust alarms will also give an early warning against engine overheating. It's not always understood that water temperature alarms only work when their sensors are immersed. If the water were suddenly to drain from the engine block, you might be none the wiser until serious, possibly terminal damage overtook your engine. That alone is sufficient reason to fit an exhaust alarm.

CHAPTER 4

The Engine Cooling System

WHEN WE CONTRIVE A SEQUENCE OF CLOSELY spaced explosions and then have hundreds of components rubbing together at the same time, no one should be astonished that things get rather hot. Unless we do something about it, the temperature will quickly rise out of control, beyond the tolerance of the various materials, bringing mechanical collapse and the distinct possibility of fire. For us, heat is both friend and pitiless enemy. We welcome its presence as an essential component of the power it bestows, but then need to get rid of its excesses as soon as possible.

In the boating world we're fortunate enough to have convenient access to an almost limitless supply of an extremely effective coolant—water.

All we have to do is harness it efficiently and our troubles will be borne away.

The hottest bits of the engine are those that enclose the combustion. In special need of protection are the cylinder heads, which are stuffed with valves, springs, and rocker arms, all potentially at risk from overheating. Although it's not obvious from the outside, the engine block and cylinder head are riddled with galleries that allow water to flow through them, getting as close to the source of the heat as possible. It's how that water gets there that distinguishes the two main methods of water cooling.

RAW-WATER COOLING

This is the most basic system (Figure 4.1). Water is pumped in from outside the boat, circulates through the engine galleries, and is pumped out again—almost always by injecting it into the exhaust. With fresh water, this isn't such a bad arrangement, but seawater—particularly warm seawater—is aggressively corrosive, and will inexorably attack the engine castings every second it remains contained within them.

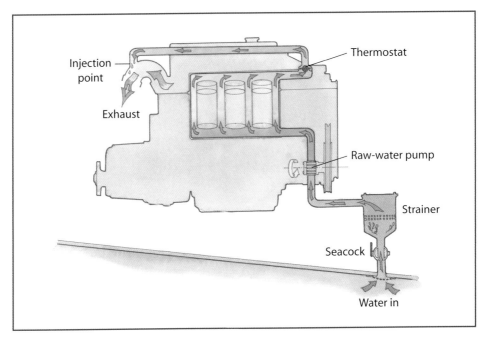

Figure 4.1   Raw-water cooling system.

Raw-water-cooled engines should be (and *used to* be) designed specifically for that purpose, with thick-walled galleries that won't quickly rust through. Marinized automotive or commercial engines, which now predominate in the real world (very few of today's engines have been designed specifically for marine use), tend to have an unacceptably brief service life if subjected to the same abuse.

For these we need a less hostile approach.

INDIRECT COOLING (HEAT EXCHANGER)

Although seawater remains the principal coolant, most marine diesel engines never come into direct contact with it. The cooling system is divided into two separate flows—one an enclosed circuit of fresh water (and additives such as antifreeze) and the other a raw-water flow that is pumped in from under the boat (Figure 4.2). The two are never mixed but come very close together in the "heat exchanger." Although more complicated, indirect cooling gives better temperature control.

Heat exchangers work by bringing two fluids—one hot, one cold—into such close proximity that one will be cooled by the other (it's a law of physics that heat always flows "downhill" from where it is to where it isn't). A good example is a car radiator, in which the temperature of the engine cooling water circulating through it is reduced by the airflow passing through the radiator. The radiator's

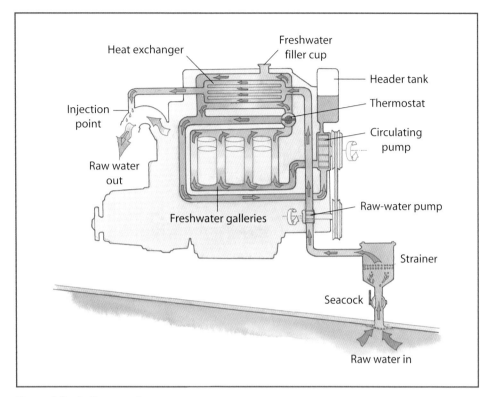

Figure 4.2 Indirect cooling system.

core is divided into a number of slender tubes or plates to maximize the area in contact with the air.

Substitute seawater for air, and a marine heat exchanger functions in a very similar way. The heated fresh water emerging from the engine block passes through a "stack" of (typically) several dozen thermally conductive tubes, which are immersed in an outer jacket containing a flow of seawater. The constantly replenished seawater cools the fresh water that eventually goes back to the engine block to continue its good work. As before, the raw water is returned to the sea via the exhaust.

KEEL COOLING

Rather than bring the raw water inside the boat to cool the freshwater circuit, keel cooling takes the fresh water outside the hull to be cooled by the waterflow. At its simplest, it might pass through a length of pipe as shown in Figure 4.3. But it could also be a section of the keel itself—most likely on steel or aluminum boats— or a specially designed heat exchanger. Keel cooling is only rarely found on pleasure craft.

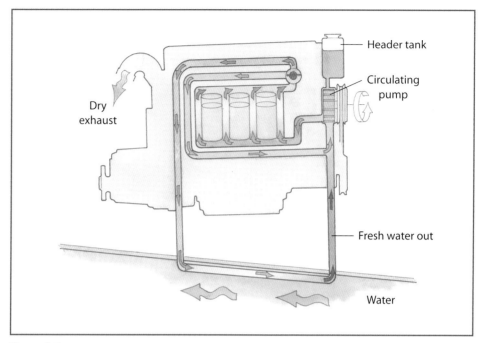

Figure 4.3   Keel cooling system.

As with all systems, there are advantages and disadvantages. On the plus side is the elimination of a raw-water pump, with all its associated headaches, such as the risk of blockage and impeller failures. Less welcome is the fact that you can no longer use the raw water to cool oil filters and the exhaust—unless you have a separate raw-water system, of course, in which case you reintroduce many of the same problems as before.

PARTS OF THE COOLING SYSTEM

THERMOSTATS

The thermostat is usually found under a dome-shaped housing like the one shown in Figure 4.4. So far we've dealt with excesses of heat, but can there be too little? Absolutely. Engines are designed to run at the temperatures they would normally achieve at their maximum output. Allowances have been made for the various components to expand accordingly. Below that point, the parts don't fit properly and will rattle about and damage themselves. So it's imperative that an engine comes up to its correct operating temperature as quickly as possible.

Figure 4.4   The thermostat is usually found under a dome-shaped housing like this. See also page 107.

In cold conditions and running under a light load, an engine might never get to that temperature if we permitted water to gambol unregulated through its galleries. This would be particularly true with raw-water cooling, since this is an open system that constantly replenishes itself with water at sea temperature.

To overcome this problem, almost all engines have thermostatic valves—commonly just called *thermostats*—strategically placed to restrict the water circulation to the cylinder head until it reaches the desired temperature. Once hot enough, the thermostat opens, and the cooling process continues unhindered through the rest of the engine. If the temperature falls, the thermostat closes, and so on.

Thermostats are ingenious little devices involving a wax-filled capsule (Figure 4.5), that expands when heated. This action forces open a spring-loaded closure, allowing the water to pass. Unfortunately, they fail in the closed position, so are always a prime suspect in cases of engine overheating.

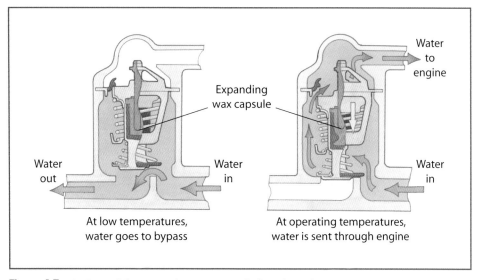

At low temperatures, water goes to bypass

At operating temperatures, water is sent through engine

Water out

Water in

Water to engine

Water in

Expanding wax capsule

Figure 4.5   Actions of the expanding wax capsule found in a thermostat.

SEACOCKS AND STRAINERS

Whether direct or indirect, effective cooling ultimately depends on having access to the water in which the boat floats—salt, fresh, or brackish depending on your location. Most stern-drive and sail-drive engines take in their raw water through their legs. For the rest of us, raw water is usually sucked in through a seacock and goes from there to a coarse filter—often called a "strainer"—that prevents water-borne debris from getting as far as the water pump.

The strainer (Figure 4.6) is often attached directly to the seacock in older designs, but modern practice raises it above the waterline to a point at which it can more conveniently be opened and cleared should a blockage occur. It helps to

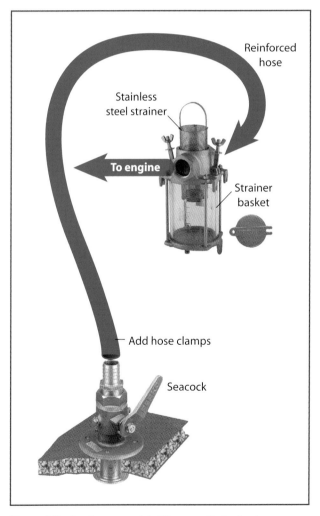

Figure 4.6   Strainer assembly. (Courtesy Perko, Inc.)

keep the hose from the seacock reasonably straight, so a flexible rod can be poked down to dislodge anything caught in it, though this is rarely possible.

A PAIR OF PUMPS

The raw water is drawn up to the engine by a self-priming pump—almost always an "impeller" pump in the engine sizes that concern us (Figure 4.7a). These get their name from the flexible impeller on which they rely. Its operation could hardly be simpler. Driven usually by a belt, the impeller rotates inside a chamber whose circular shape is distorted inward by a carefully shaped cam. The action of this distortion creates a partial vacuum that draws the water in.

Impeller pumps are water lubricated and must never be allowed to run dry for more than a few seconds. If they do, they will rapidly overheat, and the impeller will be damaged or even destroyed.

On raw-water-cooled engines, the main cooling water pump is all that's needed. However, indirect systems must also have a circulating pump (Figure 4.7b) to keep the freshwater coolant moving around its enclosed circuit. Circulating pumps are usually of the centrifugal type, in which curved impeller blades fling the water toward the outside of the pump's chamber, thereby ejecting it through the outlet.

Since circulating pumps remain permanently immersed, the ability to self-prime is irrelevant. And, except for the bearings, they have no components that rub together, so they typically give thousands of hours of service without attention.

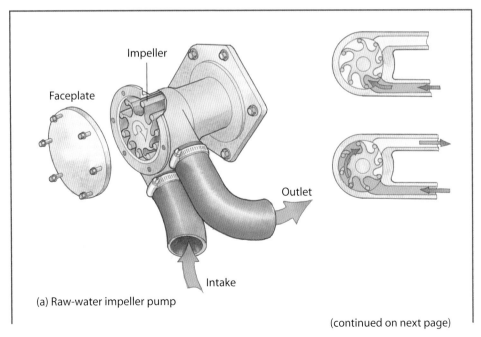

(a) Raw-water impeller pump

(continued on next page)

Figure 4.7 Cooling water pumps.

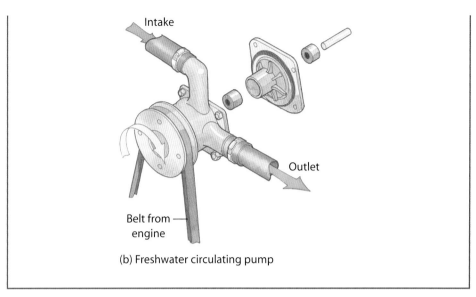

Intake

Outlet

Belt from
engine

(b) Freshwater circulating pump

Figure 4.7   (continued)

CHAPTER 5

The Electrical System

T O HAND START A DIESEL WAS ONCE NORMAL practice, but not today. Very few modern engines now have this facility. Even those that do regard it as an emergency procedure, to be used only in the event of a dead battery. The disappearance of what many would consider a useful backup can be attributed to the commercial pressures to save costs and weight, general increases in engine size, and the improved reliability of electrical systems. Though we might lament the passing of the trusty starting handle, we must accept the fact that most of us have become wholly reliant on electricity.

ELECTRICAL CIRCUITS

GROUND RETURN

In order to function, our DC (direct current) electrical systems must form a loop, known as a "circuit." There will be a power source (a battery in our case) and an electrical "load," say, a light bulb. The current flows from the positive terminal of the battery along one side of the circuit, lights the bulb, and flows back down the other side to the negative terminal. The two sides of the circuit are aptly called positive and negative (Figure 5.1a).

Almost without exception, boat engine installations have "ground return" circuits (Figure 5.1b) very much like those found in cars. The positive "hot" feed for each load travels along individual electrical cables as in the simple accompanying diagram, but in the car the negative return uses the conductive bodywork to complete the circuit back to the battery. The battery and the various loads—lights, starter motor, wipers, and so on—are all "grounded" to the bodywork, thereby connecting their negatives together.

Boats usually make use of their engine blocks in exactly the same manner. The negative terminal of the battery is connected to the block via a heavy wire. The starter motor, alternator, and such things as the oil pressure and temperature sensors are all attached directly to the engine and are therefore grounded through their casings to the negative side of the battery via that heavy wire between block and battery. Most of the other wires you will see on the engine will be positive.

The illustration shows only the starting, charging, and monitoring circuits. In reality, the engine circuitry can be complicated. Mercifully, it's usually supplied in the form of a ready-made wiring "loom" (also called a harness) that need only be taken from its box and plugged in. Of course, this still leaves other items to be supplied and fitted by the boatbuilder. These include the batteries (usually more than one) and switches and fuses to isolate and protect the system.

INSULATED RETURN

Although ground return via the engine block is an agreeably economical arrangement, it has its downsides. The most serious is the risk of electrolytic corrosion that can arise if a poor connection forces the current to "leak" out and seek an alternative path back to ground. Steel- and aluminum-hulled boats are notably vulnerable—the latter most particularly.

The solution is to isolate the engine from the vessel's metal hull (in an electrical sense) by using nonconductive engine mounts (Figure 5.1c). Since electricity always follows the path of least resistance, the heavy cable connecting the engine block to the negative battery terminal is a much better path to ground than the portion of the hull to which the engine is attached, thanks to the nonconducting mounts.

And since only steel or aluminum hulls would work similarly to the bodywork of an automobile—that is, serving as a common ground for all electrical components (fiberglass is a poor conductor)—and since, as we've already noted, this could be disastrous for a metal hull, USCG regulations require that the hull absolutely NOT be used for ground return of DC circuits. Regulations follow:

§ 111.05–11 Hull return.
(a) A vessel's hull must not carry current as a conductor except for the following systems:
   (1) Impressed current cathodic protection systems.
   (2) **Limited and locally grounded systems, such as a battery system for engine starting that has a one-wire system and the ground lead connected to the engine.** [emphasis added]
   (3) Insulation level monitoring devices if the circulation current does not exceed 30 milliamperes under the most unfavorable conditions.
   (4) Welding systems with hull return except vessels subject to 46 CFR Subchapter D.

Consequently, all DC circuits aboard will use a pair of wires, one for positive and one for the negative return. Most often, any overload protection—fuses or circuit breakers—will be in the positive side only, though some builders increase the level of protection by using double-pole breakers that interrupt both sides of the circuit (Figure 5.2).

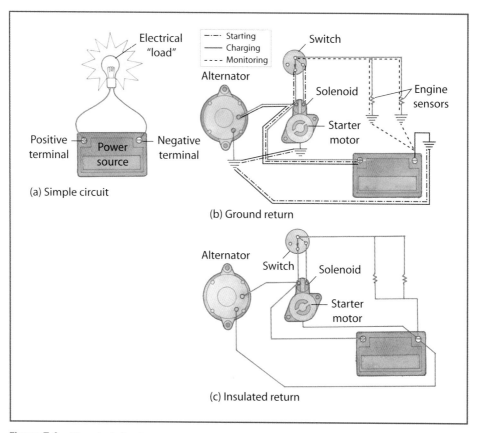

Figure 5.1   Electrical circuits.

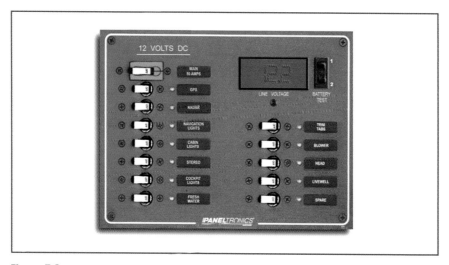

Figure 5.2   DC circuit breaker panel. (Courtesy Paneltronics)

ALTERNATORS

Batteries are like savings accounts. You can only draw out what's already been put in. Boats lying dockside can take advantage of shore-powered battery chargers, but once away from their berths they become self-dependent. More accurately, they become dependent on their engines, which, in addition to propulsion, provide a potent source of electrical power. The particular instrument of this beneficence is the alternator—a remarkably compact device in which a magnetized rotor spins within a magnetic field, the spinning being done by a belt from an engine pulley (Figure 5.3).

Batteries both deliver and are charged by DC currents, so it might seem paradoxical that, as the word implies, alternators produce alternating (AC) currents, which must be converted to DC before they're of any use. The process of this conversion is known as "rectification" and is accomplished by a nest of diodes (think of diodes as electrical one-way valves), usually built into the alternator. Also included in that general circuitry is the "regulator" that controls the charging voltage to the batteries.

BETTER CHARGING

A problem specific to sailing boats is that they don't spend much time under power. This often prevents them from charging their batteries adequately. Unfortunately, the relatively crude charging systems that come with standard alterna-

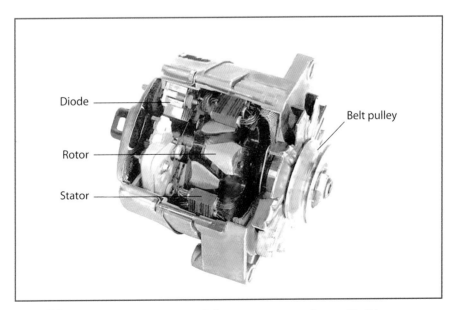

Figure 5.3   Cutaway of Delco-designed alternator now manufactured by Wagner Products Company. (Courtesy Wagner Products Company)

tors are borrowed from automotive technology and aren't very efficient at making the best of brief charging opportunities.

To overcome this, many owners fit what are commonly called "smart" regulators (or "smart chargers"—a term that risks confusion with AC-powered battery chargers). Whereas the basic regulators are simple devices whose output voltage is pre-set within a narrow band, a smart regulator imposes a sophisticated control regime that matches alternator output to the various stages in the charging process. The more advanced smart regulators also adjust the settings to suit different battery types. As well as improving the rate of charge, this more sympathetic approach helps extend battery life.

Before upgrading an existing system, it's important to ensure that any new regulator is compatible with your alternator. It's also worth noting that, in order to fit some smart regulators, the old regulator must be removed entirely. Others work in conjunction with the original, leaving it in place as a potential back-up.

TYPES OF BATTERIES

Not all batteries are intended to do the same job, and very few can do every job. To understand why this is so, it's helpful to have a basic knowledge of how they work. A battery cell (there are six cells to a 12V battery) contains a number of alternating plates, half of them positive and the other half negative. The plates are made of lead in the form of an open grid, and the holes in the grid are filled with the active constituents—lead paste in the negative and lead dioxide in the positive. The plates have separators between them to prevent them from touching and are immersed in a liquid "electrolyte" of diluted sulfuric acid.

This describes a "lead-acid" battery in a charged condition. When a loaded circuit is applied, the electrolyte combines with the materials in both plates, gradually transforming them into lead sulfate. It is this electrochemical process that releases the electrical energy through the battery's terminals. Recharging the battery involves applying an external current (from a charger) to the plates, reversing the process—that's to say converting the lead sulfate back to pure lead and lead dioxide respectively. Batteries or cells that will no longer return to their charged state are commonly said to be "sulfated."

It's that phrase, "gradually transforming" that gives a clue as to why not all batteries can perform all tasks. Nothing happens immediately in batteries, and yet there are times when we need them to release lots of energy very quickly. Starting an engine is the obvious example. The starter motor demands a tremendous output from the battery over just a few seconds. To satisfy this voracious appetite, starting batteries have a large number of thin plates (Figure 5.4a). These present the maximum area of active material to the electrolyte, thus speeding the chemical reaction.

However, if you were to use the same batteries to satisfy longer-term domestic and navigational demands, they would soon fail. No batteries like being "deep cycled," and starting batteries, with their fragile plates, are the least tolerant. Deep-cycle batteries have much stouter plates (Figure 5.4b). They can be discharged further and cycled more often but are not designed to produce that quick burst needed to start engines.

That's why many boats carry dedicated battery banks—one for engine starting and another for general service.

See Chapter 12 for battery maintenance.

WARNING

When lead-acid batteries are charged (Figure 5.5), hydrogen gas bubbles out of the electrolyte. The quantities are usually small but can pose a danger if the charge rate is vigorous or the battery becomes overcharged. This is because hydrogen is a flammable gas, which, when mixed in the right proportions with oxygen in the atmosphere, can explode. To prevent hydrogen from building up in enclosed compartments, battery boxes should always be vented to the open air.

While nearly all marine batteries are technically "lead-acid," we actually have more than one type. There are the traditional wet-cell (also called "flooded"), which have been the norm for over a hundred years, and the newer gel-cell and absorbed glass mat (AGM) batteries. Even the basic wet-cell comes in two styles: serviceable, and maintenance-free. Both are filled with liquid electrolyte and though either will work essentially as well, most experienced owners, captains, and marine mechan-

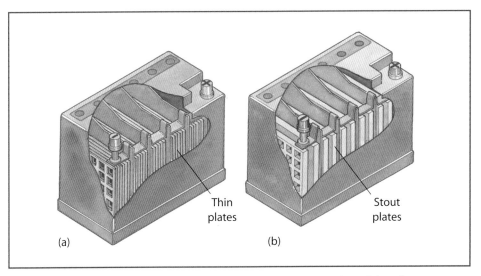

Thin plates

Stout plates

(a)   (b)

Figure 5.4   Types of batteries. (a) Starting batteries have a large number of thin plates. (b) Deep-cycle batteries have fewer, stouter plates.

ics prefer serviceable batteries because they allow us to add water to the cells when necessary (as suggested in Chapter 12) and, perhaps more important, they allow us to check the specific gravity of the electrolyte with a hydrometer, which is the most accurate means of determining a battery's state of charge.

Gel-cell and AGM batteries typically cost twice as much as a premium wet-cell. However they store very well and do not tend to sulfate or degrade as quickly or as easily as wet-cells. There is minimal chance of a hydrogen gas explosion or corrosion when using these batteries, which makes them the safest lead-acid batteries you can use. Gel-cell and some AGM batteries are more sensitive in regard to their charging rate, so if you "upgrade" from wet-cell batteries, you may need to upgrade your charging system as well.

If you are interested in specifics, AGM construction allows the electrolyte to be suspended in close proximity to the plates' active material. In theory, this improves both the discharge and recharge efficiency. Actually, AGMs are an improved variant of the valve regulated lead-acid (VRLA) batteries (the improvement is the fiberglass mat that keeps the absorbed electrolyte in better contact with the plates with none of the "sloshing" or spillage that's possible with liquid electrolyte). VRLA is the technical designation for the batteries we call "maintenance-free." These are often mistakenly called *sealed* batteries, but this term is not accurate; a sealed battery would be a safety hazard as a result of overpressure risks when overcharging, and there is always a safety valve present, hence the name valve-regulated. AGM batteries can be designed for both engine starting and deep-cycle applications. They are particularly good as deep-cycle batteries and deliver their best performance if recharged before the battery drops below the 50%

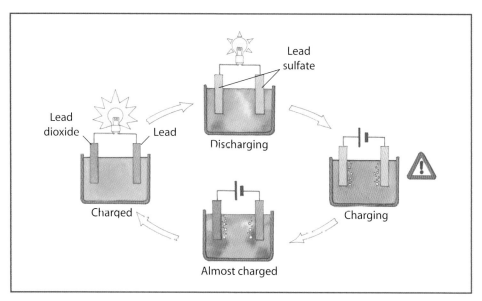

Figure 5.5 Battery charging/discharging.

discharge rate. If AGM batteries are discharged to a rate of 100%, however, their effective life will still be on the order of 300-plus cycles.

Gel-cell batteries are similar to the AGM style because the electrolyte is suspended, but they are also different because technically the AGM battery is still considered to be a wet-cell. The electrolyte in a gel-cell has a silica additive that causes it to set up or stiffen; in other words, to gel. Note that the recharge voltages on this type of cell are lower than the other styles of lead-acid battery and this is probably the most sensitive cell in terms of adverse reactions to over-voltage charging. Gel-cell batteries are best used in VERY DEEP-cycle applications and may last a bit longer in hot environment applications, which makes them quite attractive for marine use. Note, however, that if the incorrect battery charger is used on a gel-cell battery poor performance and premature failure is certain.

ENGINE STARTING

Starter motors are robust but otherwise conventional DC motors. They generally fall into one of two categories. Both work by engaging a small gear—a "pinion"—with teeth cut in the engine's flywheel. As the starter motor turns, so does the flywheel, and, hopefully, the engine springs into life. It's the manner in which the pinion engages that distinguishes between types. If the solenoid is mounted directly on the starter motor, the motor almost certainly pre-engages.

The first type are known as "inertia" starter motors (Figure 5.6). In these the pinion is free to move along helical grooves cut in the motor's shaft. When the shaft turns, the first action of the pinion is to spin out along the shaft to engage with the flywheel, which it then turns. Once the engine is turning faster than the motor, the pinion retracts.

Then there are "pre-engaged" starter motors (Figures 5.7 and 5.8). Here a solenoid-actuated arm engages the pinion with the flywheel before the motor begins to turn. This somewhat gentler approach is a lot kinder on the various mechanisms. If the solenoid is mounted directly on the starter motor, you can be almost

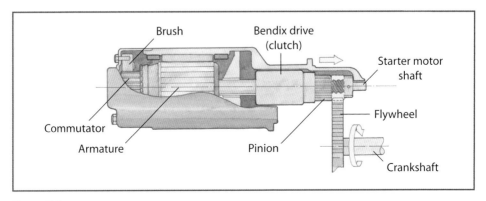

Figure 5.6   Inertia-type starter motor.

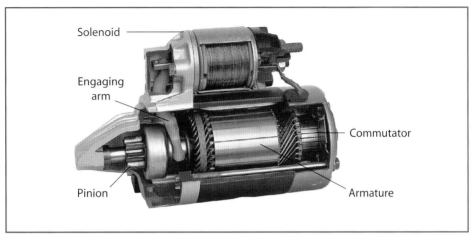

Figure 5.7   Cutaway of a pre-engaged starter motor. (Courtesy Technolab SA; www.technolab.org)

certain that it pre-engages. If it's mounted remotely, it's probably an inertia-type motor.

Whatever the means of engagement, starter motors are powerful devices that consume lots of current—albeit for a very short time. This heavy amperage draw requires heavy supply cables from the battery. Since the engine and its controls are often some distance apart, the solenoid also serves as the main switching gear. The task of energizing the solenoid from the engine ignition switch is much less demanding, so considerably lighter cables can be run from the ignition switch.

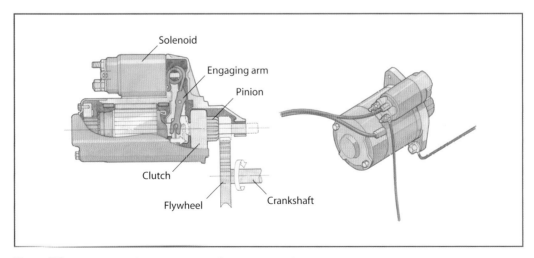

Figure 5.8   Cutaway and exterior views of a pre-engaged starter motor.

STOPPING THE ENGINE

The mechanical stop control is a small lever on the injection pump. On smaller engines, this is often actuated by pull-cables similar to those found on bicycle brakes. Larger engines use some form of electrical control—often another solenoid (Figure 5.9).

Diesels whose ancestries go back to automotive roots are usually stopped by turning off the ignition key—as they would have been in the car, van, or truck from whence they came. This is only possible because there's a solenoid-controlled valve inside the injection pump, which requires an electric current to allow the engine to run. When you switch off the power the solenoid relaxes, the valve closes, and the engine stops.

Other engines do exactly the opposite. The solenoid is inactive while the engine is running, but, on command, comes to life to pull the stop lever and shut it down. With these you will find a dedicated stop button on the control panel, or the ignition key must be turned deliberately (and usually counterclockwise) to the OFF position.

W A R N I N G

Before you operate any diesel engine, it's very important to identify the appropriate stopping procedure. Turning a key prematurely can do serious damage to the alternator.

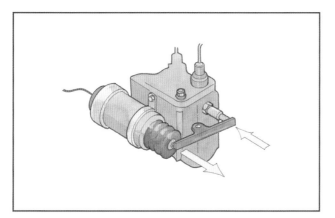

Figure 5.9   Solenoid stop for fuel injection pump.

CHAPTER 6

The Lubrication System

ALL TYPES OF COMBUSTION ENGINES NEED oil to lubricate their bearings, but the exceptionally high loads inflicted on diesels make it even more important. The greatest favor you can do a diesel engine is to be fastidious with its lubrication—which means keeping the levels topped up and replacing the oil and filters at regular intervals. Attend to this conscientiously and you will extend its life by years. Neglect these simple duties and you will soon pay the price in terms of reduced performance and expensive repairs.

Rightly described as the "lifeblood of engines," the first purpose of the oil is to reduce friction by lubricating the bearings. But it does much more than that. It also helps maintain pressure in the cylinders, inhibits corrosion, and flushes the engine of the various deposits that arise from combustion and the reducible—but never quite escapable—wear to the mechanism. These will include soot, sludge, silicon, metallic particles, and compounds arising from burning the oil itself. They are held in suspension until the oil passes through the filter, which—hopefully—removes them.

A reservoir of engine oil is carried in the crankcase, which also houses the lubricating pump—usually of rotary or gear type. The pump's job is to distribute the oil through a series of ducts and galleries to those areas in need of lubrication. If your engine has an oil pressure gauge, then it's the feed pressure at the main crankshaft bearings that's being monitored. Exceptionally low pressure is one sign that your engine is wearing out.

Turbocharged engines and the turbochargers themselves are especially demanding. The higher power outputs place tremendous loads on the bearings. To appreciate the enormity of the task, one only has to remember that failure in just a single component can bring the whole engine to its knees (Figure 6.1).

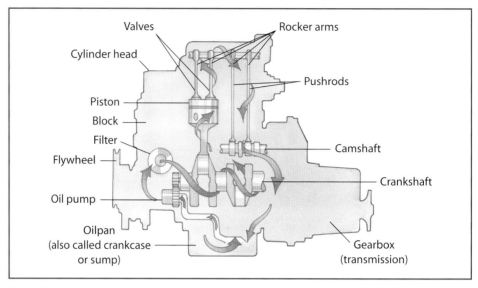

Figure 6.1   Engines are entirely reliant on efficient oil circulation.

WHAT IS LUBRICATING OIL?

The majority of engine oils on the market are refined from crude oil. But mineral oils alone aren't robust enough to cope with modern diesels, so the basic oil is fortified with additives. These might include dispersants to keep contaminants in suspension, detergents to help clean deposits from the mechanisms, and corrosion inhibitors to control rust and counteract the acids formed from the sulfur that occurs naturally in diesel fuel.

Then there are synthetic oils. These are more expensive but offer better performance and an extended service life—in other words, a longer period between oil changes. Although the word *synthetic* conjures up images of something very exotic, most are not a million miles removed from the natural product. The type we would use are synthesized hydrocarbons whose molecular structures have been designed for lubricating diesel engines. And, since they don't rely on a refining process to eliminate unwanted compounds, they contain fewer impurities.

Synthetic oils will tolerate higher temperatures than petroleum oils. Also, there's a difference in the way they "burn off." In petroleum oil the molecules vary in size. As the temperature rises, the smaller molecules burn off first, leaving the larger ones behind. This alters the characteristics of the oil. With synthetic oils the molecules are all identical. If burn-off occurs, the essential characteristics of the oil remain the same.

Hydrocarbon-based synthetic oils can be mixed with ordinary oils. Indeed, you will see for sale "semi-synthetic" oils, which are exactly that—a mix of standard and synthetic, and actually not a bad choice for many marine diesels. Other types may be incompatible. Check before you change.

And never skimp on your oil. Buy the best you can. The higher the performance of the engine, the better must be the quality. Two organizations test and categorize oil types. The first (and of greatest concern to those of us in North America) is the American Petroleum Institute (API), which uses the code letter "C" (compression) to indicate a diesel oil, followed by a second letter (and number) denoting the standard of that oil. API CJ-4 is the highest grade at the moment, but this has been specifically formulated to help 2007 model-year engines meet highway emissions standards when used in conjunction with the low-sulfur fuels also now required for on-road use. It will work in marine engines, including older models, but the currently higher sulfur content of marine fuels may require a different oil-change interval. If you use the new CJ lube oil, consult your engine manufacturer regarding recommended change intervals. And keep in mind that as the sulfur levels of marine (and other off-road) fuels are reduced, first to 500 ppm in June 2007 and then to 15 ppm in June 2010, manufacturers' recommendations may be revised to match the new realities. Note, however, that in the meantime, the older grades such as API CH or even CF should be more than adequate for most purposes.

The second body is the Brussels-based Association des Constructeurs Européens d'Automobiles (ACEA) whose diesel categories start with "D" or "PD" and might be followed by E2 for a standard performance level oil or E3 for higher performance.

The word "might" in that last sentence is significant. As development progresses and new products are introduced, older grades become obsolete. You may therefore find that your engine manual is asking for a grade of oil that no longer exists—in which case, ask the suppliers for the nearest equivalent. If in doubt, use a higher specification than necessary.

OIL FILTERS

There's little point in changing the oil if you don't change the filter as well. On engines within the size range that concerns us, virtually all oil filters are of the screw-on cartridge type that only take a couple of minutes to replace. Their cost is minuscule compared to that of the engine, so don't be tempted by false economies.

The oil filter housing usually contains the pressure relief valve—not something you usually have to worry about. Its job is to divert the oil back into the sump if the filter becomes so clogged as to prevent normal flow (Figure 6.2).

Figure 6.2 Oil filters need regular replacement.

OIL PUMP

This is the heart of the engine lubrication system. The pump lives in the bottom of the crankcase and can be of various types. Perhaps the most common is the trochoid type shown here (Figure 6.3).

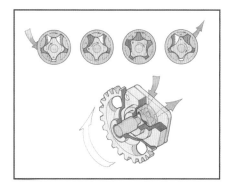

Figure 6.3   Trochoid oil pump. The pump action is simpler than it looks.

As long as the oil is changed regularly, lubrication pumps need almost no maintenance. Normally, by the time they wear out, the rest of the engine is in even worse shape.

GEARBOX LUBRICATION

The absence of combustion by-products might make lubricating the gearbox (transmission) a simpler matter, but it's certainly no less important. Some gearboxes use the same grade oil as the engine. Others prefer automatic transmission fluid. Consult the manual before you change the oil. Also check on the correct way to use the dipstick. The oil level reading is often taken without screwing the dipstick down—in other words, with the bottom of the threads resting on the casing. This means that you can't rely on the mark when you first withdraw the dipstick. It must be wiped clean and reinserted only as far as the threads to yield a proper reading. Note also that some gearboxes require that the fluid level be measured only after starting the engine, while others can be read at any time—be sure to consult the manual.

OIL COOLERS

These are seawater-cooled heat exchangers, similar in principle to the one used in the cooling water circuit (Figure 6.4). One of the penalties of wringing more and more power out of smaller and smaller engines is that operating temperatures tend to rise. It's worth reflecting on the fact that many engines might have three or four heat exchangers—all of which should be inspected and serviced regularly.

Pay particular attention to the sacrificial anodes, if there are any. If galvanic corrosion were to eat through the cooling tubes, you would be sending both oil and water to places where they don't belong. The outcome will be interesting—and certainly expensive.

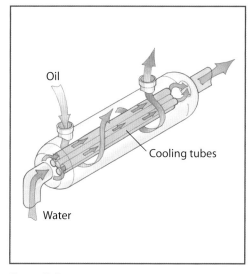

Oil

Cooling tubes

Water

Figure 6.4   Oil cooler. Another form of heat exchanger. Keeping the oil cool helps extend engine life.

CHAPTER 7

The Transmission and Drive Train

O NE OF THE MOST IMPORTANT TRUTHS we must face is that no matter how much power an engine may develop, it does us absolutely no good at all until we can turn its torque, which is what we call the rotational force the engine produces, into thrust, the push that propels the boat. To accomplish this we need a drive train.

DIRECT DRIVE VIA GEARBOX, SHAFT, AND PROPELLER

In an age of advancing mechanical complexity, this straightforward approach might seem rather old-fashioned, but it offers the considerable virtues of simplicity and reliability. It remains the firm favorite among sailing yachts and the more traditional types of power craft, but has lost some ground among modern motor vessels.

It seems almost superfluous to describe its basic elements. Power from the engine emerges from the gearbox, also known as the transmission, and is transmitted down a shaft to the propeller. A waterproof gland ("stuffing box") is needed to keep the water out of the hull, and there must be a bearing immediately forward of the propeller to support the shaft (Figure 7.1).

GEARBOXES

An engine's power is of no use unless it can be delivered to the propeller shaft in a controlled and proper way. The responsibility for achieving this rests with the transmission—more commonly called the gearbox (Figure 7.2).

The gearbox has two distinct functions. The rotational output from modern diesels is usually too fast to be passed on unmodified. On all but the lightest, swiftest boats, a large propeller turning slowly is more efficient than a smaller one

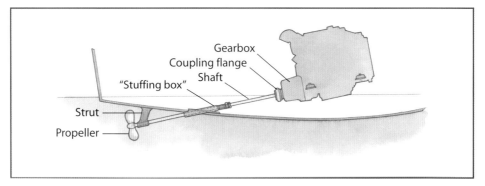

Figure 7.1   A typical shaft and strut installation—simple but robust.

turning quickly. The first task of the gearbox is therefore to act as a "reduction gear." The amount by which the revolutions are reduced is expressed as a ratio between input and output. For example a gear ratio of 3:1 tells us that the crankshaft will turn three times for every single turn of the propeller shaft; 2:1 means it goes round twice, and so on (Figure 7.3).

However, the time when we become the most aware of a gearbox's function is when we're maneuvering under power. It allows us to motor ahead and astern, and also to remain stationary with the engine running. Along with the throttle and steering, it's one of our three primary controls.

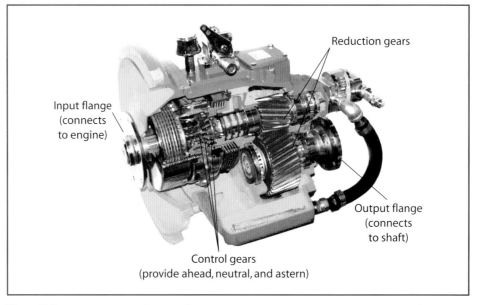

Figure 7.2   Cutaway view of a typical marine gear. (Courtesy Transmission Marine; Bob Armstrong photo)

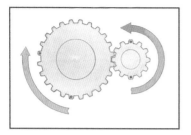

Figure 7.3 With a gear ratio of 2:1 the larger gear has twice as many teeth as the smaller one.

Marine gearboxes are fundamentally different from automotive types. Their gears are permanently meshed and (usually) turn whenever the engine is running. An internal clutch—or clutches—of one sort or another determines the manner in which the power is transmitted to the propeller shaft coupling. They fall into one of two distinct categories: "mechanical" or "hydraulic." These two self-explanatory terms describe how the transmissions are controlled—not the basic principles of how they work. Mechanical gearboxes are operated mechanically. Hydraulic gearboxes use an oil pump and hydraulic pressure to move the various internal bits about—a necessity in larger sizes in which the loads can become considerable. In fact, since the only manual work entails operating valves, it's not surprising that hydraulic gearboxes are the lightest to control, regardless of size.

Twin-Shaft Transmission

This is a very common type of transmission, and probably the easiest to describe and understand (Figure 7.4).

In neutral, the forward gear (F) and the reverse gear (R) both freewheel on the output shaft. The two gears (A) and (B) are permanently fixed to the input shaft but (A) is never engaged directly with (R).

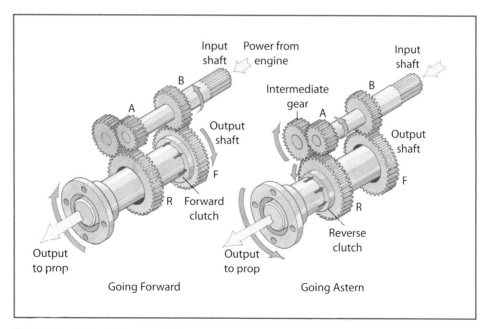

Figure 7.4 Twin-shaft transmission.

To go forward, a clutch moves against (F) and locks it to the output shaft—that's to say, it prevents it freewheeling. The drive from the input shaft now acts through (B) to turn (F) and the output shaft in the opposite direction.

To go astern, the forward clutch disengages, freeing (F), and the reverse clutch moves against (R) to lock it to the output shaft as before. Now the drive from the output shaft transfers power though (A) and the intermediate gear to turn (R) and the output shaft in the same direction as the input shaft.

Planetary or Epicyclic Transmission

This mechanism earns its name from its resemblance to our solar system—a "sun" at center with a number of "planets" in orbit around it. Although baffling at first glance, the way it works is really very simple and offers a number of options from just a single device (Figure 7.5).

The input drive from the engine is through the sun gear (1), which always turns in the same direction. Around the sun gear are arranged three pairs of intermediate planet gears (2) mounted on a "planet carrier" (3). The planet carrier can be connected by clutches to either the output shaft (4), which emerges from the after end of the gearbox, or the "annulus" (5). The planet gears turn freely and mesh with both the sun gear and the inside surface of the annulus. The annulus can also rotate around its axis.

Let's now imagine a system of clutches and brakes (not all are shown) each capable of locking components in place or together, and see how the planetary gear would perform in three different circumstances:

A. Firstly, if the sun gear were locked to the planet carrier the whole assembly would rotate in the same direction and at the same speed—i.e., the gear ratio would be 1:1. This, of course, is too fast for most boats, so some kind of reduction is called for.

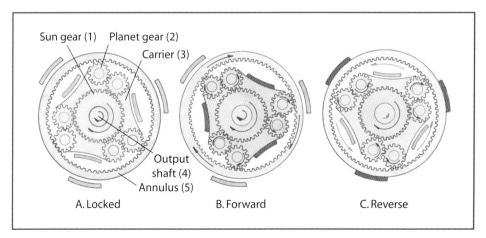

Sun gear (1)   Planet gear (2)
Carrier (3)
Output shaft (4)
Annulus (5)
A. Locked   B. Forward   C. Reverse

Figure 7.5 Epicyclic gearing (see text).

B. In the second situation, the planet carrier is disconnected from the sun gear and immobilized. A clutch locks the annulus to the output shaft. Now, when the sun gear turns, the drive is transmitted by the planet gears to the annulus (and thereby the output shaft), which rotates in the same direction but more slowly. On most boats, this would be forward gear.

C. To go astern, we must look at the third situation. The planet carrier is locked to the output shaft, but not to the sun gear. The annulus is immobilized, either with a clutch or band brake. This time when drive is applied, the planet gears roll around the inside of the annulus, slower and in the opposite direction. This is reverse gear.

These examples describe principles that could be applied differently in other circumstances—not least at the heart of automatic gearboxes in road vehicles. And a well-known American marine gearbox uses a pair of planetary gear systems in tandem. The first gives forward (A) and reverse (C) while the second system reduces the forward gear ratio as in (B). Unfortunately, the engineering complexity does add to costs—one of the reasons for the type's declining popularity.

SHAFT COUPLINGS

The most basic type of coupling is simply a pair of matching steel flanges—one on the gearbox output and the other on the propeller shaft. These are bolted together face-to-face and form a rigid joint between the two.

But bear in mind that almost all engines sit on flexible rubber mounts. These are designed to absorb vibration and inhibit the propagation of structure-borne noise. They also allow the engine to move a little, particularly from side to side. The only way this movement can be accommodated by a rigid shaft is for the shaft itself to flex. This translates as increased loads on the whole stern gear assembly and—naturally—a route through which more vibrations will find their way into the hull. So, it makes sense to introduce at least some flexibility into the coupling.

Flexible Couplings and Constant Velocity Joints   Flexible shaft couplings come in many shapes and sizes. The most compact—and the least expensive—can be inserted into an existing coupling without further modification. The shaft will protrude a little farther aft but this is rarely of any consequence. A coupling of this type is shown here (Figure 7.6).

A more elaborate coupling comprises a pair of automotive type constant velocity joints connected by a short intermediate shaft (Figure 7.7). It also incorporates a thrust bearing at

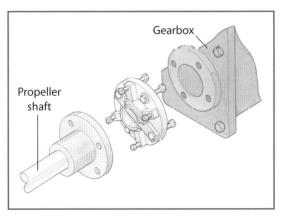

Figure 7.6   Semi-flexible coupling.

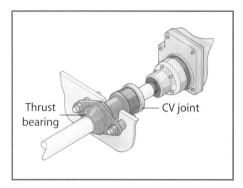

Figure 7.7   A CV joint will reduce vibration and entirely remove the thrust loads from the engine.

Thrust bearing

CV joint

the prop shaft end, relieving the engine of the fore-and-aft loads it would normally have to resist. This means the engine can sit on even softer mounts than before, further dampening those unwanted vibrations.

Although such an arrangement could be retrofitted, it would be better if it were part of the original design, since a strong transverse member has to be included in the structure to take those thrust loads. Designers are sometimes attracted by these couplings because the misalignment they will tolerate can be deliberately used to install the engine and shaft at different angles.

STUFFING BOXES

This is an area that has seen a flurry of development over the last few years, with a number of proprietary stern glands appearing on the market (see next section). That said, an enormous number of the traditional packed glands ("stuffing boxes") are still doing sterling work.

Packed glands are nothing more than a pair of concentric cylinders, one inside the other. The way they work is best explained by the accompanying illustration (Figure 7.8). Basically, three or four rings of packing material are compressed between an internal shoulder (machined inside the outer casing) and the end of the inner compressor tube which is pressed down onto the packing, either by a threaded collar, or as shown here, with a couple of bolts pulling down on protruding flanges. The latter is the better arrangement, being easier to adjust and presenting less chance of straining the gland—even wrenching it away—as you do so.

The packing material is most commonly of square-sectioned braided flax (Figure 7.9), but there are also a number of synthetic materials, all claiming their own advantages. The gland is lubricated with a water-resistant grease—often supplied by a "remote greaser"—and, to a great extent, by the water itself. For that last reason, it's important to note that packed glands are intended to leak. Not copiously, however. Two or three drips a minute is quite enough.

Packed glands are often attached to the stern tube with a short length of rubber hose. This allows the gland to move with the engine, reducing the side loads

WARNING

Packed glands should never be overtightened. If they are they will run hot and cause serious wear to the shaft. After a period under power, stop the engine and feel the gland. It should be cool to the touch.

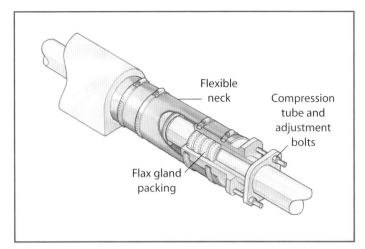

Flexible neck

Compression tube and adjustment bolts

Flax gland packing

Figure 7.8   Stuffing box.

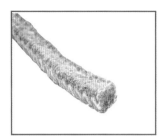

Figure 7.9   Flax packing. (Courtesy YC Industries)

that would otherwise occur. Clearly, failure of the hose would cause catastrophic leakage. Bearing in mind the trifling costs involved, it makes sense to replace it, and the hose clips that secure it, every time the shaft is drawn.

Modern Shaft Seals

There are a number of alternatives to old-fashioned packed glands, and it's easy to understand why these stern gland upstarts are gaining ground. Once fitted and adjusted, they need less attention, and are entirely drip-free. They are also a lot less messy than the older variety.

To keep the water at bay, modern stern glands rely on one of two principles. The first are "lip seals" (Figure 7.10a), similar in many ways to the oil seals found at each end of your engine's crankshaft. A flexible rubber lip bears on the shaft, pointing upstream toward the water so the hydrostatic pressure works to keep it in contact. The water also lubricates the seal, though some manufacturers advise squirting in tiny amounts of grease periodically to give it a helping hand.

The second type of modern stern glands are known as "face seals" (Figure 7.10b). With these a graphite ring presses against a stainless steel collar that rotates with the shaft. Contact between the ring and the collar is maintained by a compressed rubber bellows that acts like a spring. Again, the lubricant is water.

It's vital to keep both lip and face seals constantly lubricated. If starved of water for more than few moments they will overheat and destroy themselves. This is rarely a problem at low speeds, since a stern gland will be permanently flooded. But above about 12 knots the water rushing past the after end of a stern tube can develop a strong enough venturi effect to literally suck it dry (Figure 7.11). The solution is to divert water from the engine's raw-water systems and inject it directly into the glands.

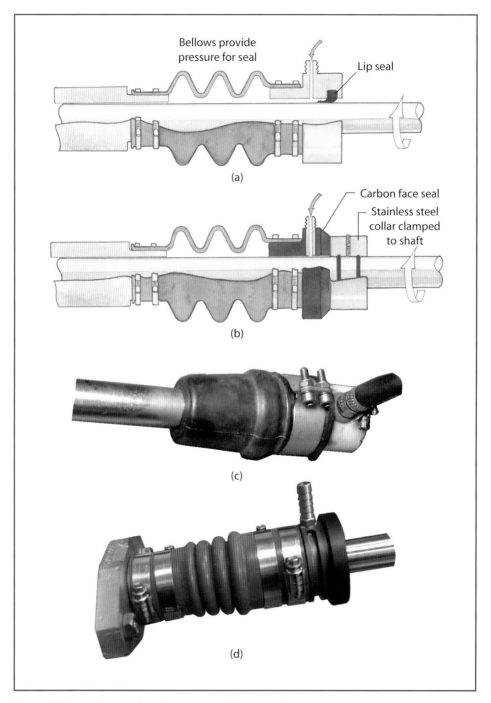

Figure 7.10   Modern shaft seals. (a) Lip seal; (b) Face seal; (c) Volvo stern gland; (d) Another example of a modern stern gland.

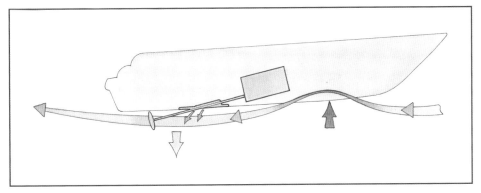

Figure 7.11 At high speeds, the venturi effect can suck the water out and cause the stern gland to run dry.

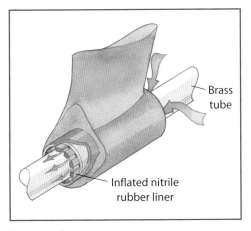

Brass tube

Inflated nitrile rubber liner

Figure 7.12 Cutless bearing.

SHAFT BEARINGS

With very few exceptions the only serious player now left in this field is the water-lubricated "cutless bearing" (Figure 7.12). And it could hardly be a simpler object.

A tube, most commonly of brass but sometimes phenolic or fiberglass, contains a fluted nitrile rubber liner. Unlikely as it might seem, the rubber is the bearing surface and the flutes are there to encourage water to flow along its length.

Apart from its admirable simplicity, the other strength of the cutless bearing is its tolerance to minor engine misalignment—unfortunately, a virtue often abused by engineers too careless to get it right. Cutless bearings are either carried in a "P bracket" or in the end of the stern tube, depending on the hull configuration. Either way, their purpose is to support the shaft just forward of the propeller.

PROPELLERS

When, in a boating context, we talk of "screws," we're often referring to propellers. And there are certainly some similarities. Both woodscrews and propellers are helical objects, which wind themselves through their respective media by rotation. But there are important differences, both in the way they work and the media in which they exist. Timber is a solid whereas water is a fluid. And, while woodscrews gain grip the farther they penetrate, there's no equivalent cumulative benefit for a propeller. In the production of thrust they rely entirely on the revolution current at any time.

So, although the analogy remains useful, let's treat it with caution and see propellers for what they really are: foils—more accurately an assemblage of two or more foils arranged symmetrically around a hub. If anything, propellers resemble sails and rudders more closely than they do screws.

Before we dig deeper into the dynamics, let's shed light on some of the terminology. On the hub somewhere will be stamped a simple code—15 × 11 RH, for example. This tells us that this particular propeller is 15 inches in diameter, has a "pitch" of 11 inches and turns "right handed." The units could also be metric, the difference hopefully being obvious.

The diameter is that of the circle swept by the blades. Pitch is the distance the propeller would move forward in one revolution if able to screw through a solid. A right-handed prop is one whose upper blades are moving to starboard when in forward gear—turning clockwise when viewed from astern (Figure 7.13).

Let's look at pitch a little closer (Figure 7.14a). Most propeller blades aren't flat, but are twisted along their length (Figure 7.14b).

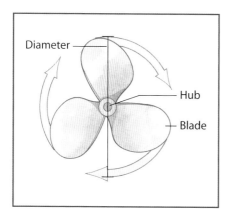

Figure 7.13 Right-handed propeller spinning in forward gear.

In conversations on this subject you'll sometimes hear people remark that the "pitch" of the blade is coarser toward the hub than it is at the tip. What the speaker really means is that the "blade angle" is coarser—and, indeed, it has to be. This is because the farther out from the hub you get, the greater the circumference that must be followed by the corresponding part of the blade. Again using our 15-inch (381 mm)

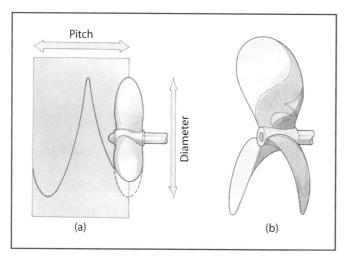

Figure 7.14 Pitch (a) and twist (b).

prop as an example, we can calculate that the part of the blade situated 2 inches (51 mm) from the center will travel around the shaft axis just over 12.5 inches (318 mm) in one revolution, while the tip will travel over 47 inches (1194 mm)—nearly four times as far. If the two had the same blade angle, that disparity would translate into a similar difference in forward movement. And, since it would be embarrassing to have the blade tips arriving at a destination before the rest of the prop, they're given a shallower angle to keep them in check. It's the even transition from shallow to steeper angles that gives the blades their characteristic twist—the twist that's essential in order to maintain constant pitch.

So, can we now assume that every turn of the prop will drive the boat forward by a distance equal to the pitch? Alas, no. Water isn't like the timber into which we earlier drove a woodscrew. It's a displaceable, yielding fluid whose antics are very difficult to predict. But it's not all bad news. Foils only work in fluids, so the very characteristics that torment us are those the propeller uses to generate thrust. Propellers can never be 100% efficient. Some of the theoretical maximum will always be lost to slip.

The bottom line is that the actual distance traveled in one revolution—known as the "advance"—can fall well short of pitch. The shortfall between pitch and advance is called "slip" (Figure 7.15) and is expressed as a percentage of pitch. And this is no small matter. The slip on a sailing yacht under power could be as much as 50%, and on a high-speed motor cruiser, perhaps half that. If a boat is heavily fouled or overloaded with gear the slip will increase dramatically.

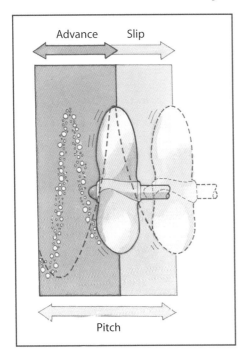

Figure 7.15 Slip.

It makes sense to try to reduce slip as much as is practicable but it is neither possible nor desirable to eliminate it entirely. Like many things in boating, it's something we must learn to live with.

Ventilation and cavitation—two demons of the propulsion world—are often confused. Ventilation (Figure 7.16a) is air being drawn down from the surface to aerate the water surrounding the propeller. Since the mix of air and water is considerably less dense than the water alone, the prop's revs increase while its thrust diminishes. Ventilation is common with outboard motors and stern drives, but is rarely a problem for props operating in solid water under the hull.

Cavitation (Figure 7.16b) is a lot less fussy where it strikes, though effects on performance are much the same. Foils work by creating low pressure on one side—the forward side in the case of propellers. If the pressure becomes too low the water will boil, even at the temperature of seawater. This creates vapor-filled voids that

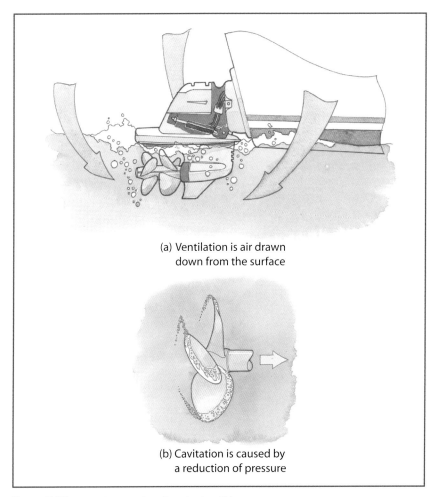

(a) Ventilation is air drawn
down from the surface

(b) Cavitation is caused by
a reduction of pressure

Figure 7.16   Ventilation (a) and cavitation (b).

can implode with amazing force, sometimes damaging the surface of the blades. This damage is usually called "cavitation burn."

Almost any prop can be made to cavitate by heavy-handed use of the throttle, but if it happens in normal service there is either damage to the prop—a bent blade perhaps—or the prop is too small or under-pitched for the engine.

Which takes us neatly to the next subject . . .

Picking the Right Prop

Here we enter dragon country, for this is a field where even computer-wielding experts get it wrong. On the face of it, the task seems straightforward enough: find the prop that best matches your boat, engine, and intended usage. The right prop should allow the engine to develop its full output, yet prevent it from over-revving.

Propellers come in all shapes and sizes. Picking the right one is more complicated than it might seem.

Unfortunately, there's no single formula that satisfies all sets of circumstances. There are too many variables. A prop that works well on one 30-footer won't necessarily deliver the goods on another—not even if they have the same engine and are similar in form and displacement. It's not unusual for new designs to be "propped" several times before a final choice is made. And it's worth persisting, since the positive effects on performance can be rewarding.

If facing the prospect of choosing a prop, everyone has to start somewhere. Imperfect though they might be, the people to consult first are the experts, meaning the manufacturers and suppliers. If it's a popular class of vessel, they may already have the answers on file. If not they will need details of the boat. These include the waterline length, waterline beam, displacement, maximum speed, and a general summary of the type—long keel, planing, multihull, whatever. Also, details of the engine: its horsepower, maximum revs, reduction ratio, and whether it's a single or twin installation. Then there will be your preferred type of prop: how many blades (Figure 7.17), normal or low-drag, fixed, folding, or feathering.

This gives some idea of the number of permutations involved. Computers can help narrow the choice, but at the end of the day science often gives way to the black art of personal judgment. And in this the person with the most experience has the best chance of getting it right.

We have talked of diameter and pitch but so far have ignored blade area. Because propellers are foils, it would be tempting to make a direct comparison with sail area, but this would be misleading since they are harnessed in very different ways. Nonetheless, the comparison stands well enough for us to appreciate that for any given prop diameter, the more area we have the better.

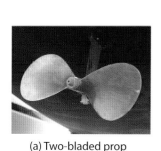  

(a) Two-bladed prop   (b) Three-bladed prop   (c) Four-bladed prop

Figure 7.17   Picking the right prop can be complicated.

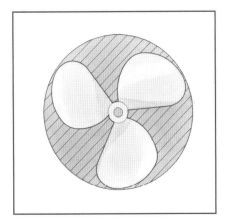

Figure 7.18   The disc area ratio (DAR) is the proportion of blade area to swept area.

To allow us to compare propellers of the same diameter we refer to the "disc area ratio" (DAR) (Figure 7.18). This is the ratio between the projected area of the blades and that of the circle they sweep. For example, a prop with a blade area of 130 in² sweeping a 200 in² circle would have a DAR of 65% (130/200 = 0.65). Clearly the larger the DAR the more grip in the water a propeller is likely to have.

While a hefty DAR might be beneficial under power, the associated drag is wholly bad news for boats under sail. Fixed props mitigate the problem by reducing their blade areas. These compromise "sailing" props have two skinny blades and a DAR of about 25%. Drag is reduced accordingly, but, as you might expect, they aren't very efficient under power, particularly in demanding conditions.

Another approach is to fit propellers that adapt to both modes. These fall into two categories: folding and feathering. When under sail, folding-prop blades pivot backward to stream in the waterflow, and are then flung open by centrifugal force once the shaft starts turning. In forward gear, the thrust serves to hold them open (Figures 7.19 and 7.20). In reverse, only the centrifugal force keeps the blades deployed, making them less efficient in that

Figure 7.19   Two-bladed folding prop.

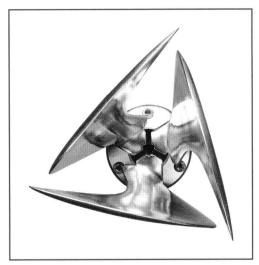

Figure 7.20   Three-bladed folding prop. (Courtesy Volvo Penta)

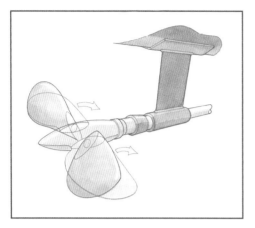

Figure 7.21 Feathering prop.

mode. Skippers soon learn to keep the revs up when applying the brakes, but a downwind approach into a marina berth still remains an entertaining experience.

Feathering props (Figures 7.21, 7.22a and b), on the other hand, have no such problem. They are just as efficient astern as they are going ahead. With the shaft immobile, the blades naturally align themselves with the waterflow. But as soon as the shaft starts to rotate—in either direction—the sideways resistance on the blades twists them to a pre-set pitch. A useful feature of feathering props is that the pitch can be adjusted if you don't get it right first time.

As always, there can be a downside. Since the blades of feathering props are often flat, it's impossible for them to have the constant pitch from root to tip described earlier. This means that feathering props are less efficient and more susceptible to cavitation—and the damage that can go with it. However this is more of a problem on some brands of feathering propellers than others—note the twist on the three-bladed feathering prop shown in Figure 7.22b, giving it fairly constant pitch.

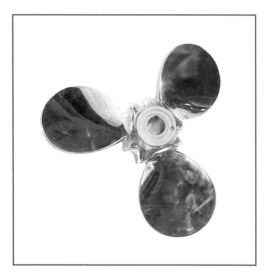

Figure 7.22a Feathering prop open (working). (Courtesy Paul F. Luke, Inc.)

Figure 7.22b Feathering prop closed (feathered). (Courtesy Paul E. Luke, Inc.)

INTEGRATED DRIVES

There are advantages in combining the entire propulsion system into a single compact unit. That way the manufacturers take the whole process under their control, ensuring there are no weaknesses or incompatibilities anywhere in the power train. The boatbuilders simply take the unit out of its box and bolt it into the place prepared for it. The engine, transmission, and final drive are installed, literally within minutes, without any of the tricky alignment procedures associated with conventional installations. Hook up the controls, fuel, and electrics, and you're ready to go.

STERN DRIVES

Otherwise known as "inboard-outboards" or "outdrives," stern drives reign supreme on small to mid-size diesel-engined craft (Figures 7.23, 7.24, and 7.25). Each complete assembly pierces and is attached to the transom, with a "drive leg" outside the hull and the engine inside. Waterproof bellows or gaskets allow the two to work together without admitting water into the boat.

The drive leg contains the gearbox and a system of bevel gears to crank the output around two 90° corners. It can also be moved from side to side to provide steering, and can be tilted up and down to reduce draft and adjust fore-and-aft trim. Needless to say, it's a complicated mechanism, one you would be very unwise to neglect.

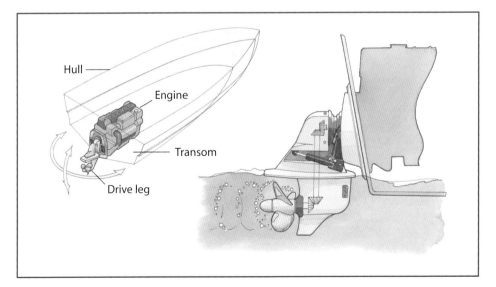

Figure 7.23   A stern drive can be used both to steer and to adjust trim.

Figure 7.24 MerCruiser Alpha Drive. (Courtesy Cummins MerCruiser)

Figure 7.25 Volvo Duoprop drive with engine. (Courtesy Volvo Penta)

"POD" SYSTEMS

Similar to stern drives in that they are steerable (though not trimmable), pods are also different in that they go through the bottom of the hull rather than through the transom. Thus they operate under the boat rather than behind it. In another similarity to stern drives, the pods are also integrated systems with self-contained raw-water intakes and spent gas exhausts, which eliminate the need for more holes in the hull. Another difference: stern-drive drive legs are largely aluminum, while the pods employ mostly stainless steel and nibral, the same corrosion-resistant nickel-bronze-aluminum alloy used in high-quality propellers. This greatly lessens the potential for underwater corrosion.

There are currently two pod systems in the marketplace: Volvo Penta's IPS, which was introduced in 2005 (Figure 7.26); and the Cummins MerCruiser version, known as Zeus, which will be widely available in 2008 (Figure 7.27), though the company started taking orders in 2007.

Both systems use dual, contra-rotating props (on concentric shafts); the IPS props face forward, while the Zeus props are more

Figure 7.26 Volvo Penta Inboard Performance System (IPS) drive. (Courtesy Volvo Penta)

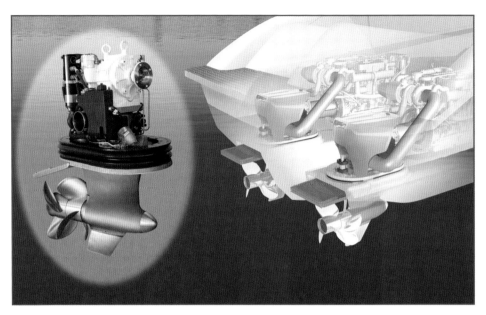

Figure 7.27   Cummins MerCruiser Zeus system. (Courtesy Cummins MerCruiser)

traditional and face aft. Both companies report evidence that the pods present a number of advantages over older drive systems in both overall efficiency—including higher top speed, faster acceleration, and reduced fuel consumption—and also in ease of handling. In the latter department, both systems also offer "joystick" (Figure 7.28) control by which the boat can be guided in close quarters maneuvers and/or held on station (despite the efforts of wind and current to displace it) by positioning the single control stick.

Pods may never totally replace the more conventional drive systems, but they are definitely a wave of the future.

Figure 7.28   Joystick control. A single joystick can maneuver the boat with either the IPS or Zeus pod propulsion systems. (Courtesy Cummins MerCruiser)

SAIL DRIVES

Popular on small to mid-size yacht auxiliaries, a "sail drive" is a relatively simple device that can neither be steered nor tilted (Figures 7.29 and 7.30). The drive leg passes through a strong rubber diaphragm that isolates the engine vibrations from the hull while keeping the water at bay. Some models have twin diaphragms with an electronic leak sensor between.

Stern drives and sail drives have their limitations. In both cases the friction in all that gearing takes its toll and there is a consequen-

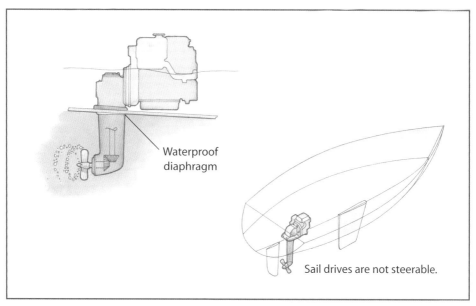

Waterproof diaphragm

Sail drives are not steerable.

Figure 7.29 Sail drive.

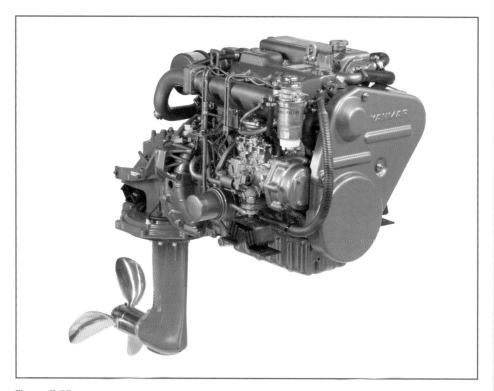

Figure 7.30 Sail drive. (Courtesy Yanmar)

tial power loss. Stern drives are found on engines of up to about 480hp (358 kW), while sail drives are only available up to perhaps 40hp (30 kW)—a commercial rather than practical limit.

WATER JETS

Instead of operating in open water, the propeller—now called an "impeller"—is placed in a duct where it sucks water through a grating in the bottom of the boat and squirts it out from the stern at great velocity. The outlet nozzle can be directed from side to side to give steering. Going astern is achieved by lowering a carefully shaped "bucket" over the outlet to reverse the flow.

Since water jets add nothing to a vessel's draft, they are excellent in shallow water (Figure 7.31). The absence of an exposed prop also makes them ideal for rescue or diving duties.

WARNING

The casings of both stern and sail drives are made predominantly of aluminum and are therefore susceptible to galvanic corrosion. Full cathodic protection should always be maintained by replacing anodes frequently.

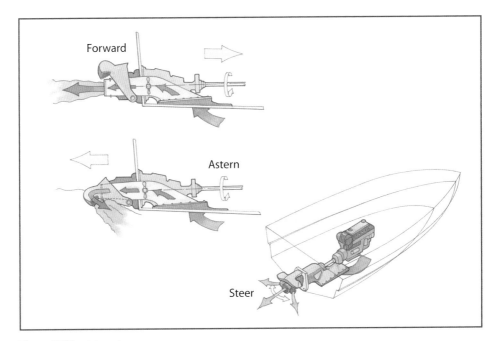

Figure 7.31   Water jets.

CHAPTER 8

Engine Controls

AS ENGINES HAVE BECOME LARGER, the means of controlling them have become more sophisticated. Although open boats with gear levers poking up through their cockpit soles can still be found, most of us are denied such simplicity because our engines and steering positions are located some distance from each other. In many instances—flybridge powerboats and deck saloon sailing yachts being notable examples—there will be two (or more) command positions, each with its own set of controls.

The full array of controls will comprise: controls needed to start and stop the engine, controls to select the appropriate gear, and controls to operate the throttle. Boats with stern drives will also need to include steering—since this is achieved by directing the thrust from the drive—and also the tilt controls that allow adjustment of a vessel's fore-and-aft trim.

The communication between helm and engine can be achieved in various ways: by push-pull cable, by a hydraulic system, electronically, or pneumatically. Very often there's a mix of methods. Even the simplest boat is likely to have electric start and stop controls with a cable operating the gears and throttle. On stern drives it's common to see electric pumps powering the hydraulic tilt rams and push-pull cables actuating the power-assisted hydraulic steering.

The attractions of hydraulic, pneumatic (air), and electronic systems are obvious. Threading small-bore pipework or electrical wiring through a boat is much easier than finding an easy path for cables, in which minimizing friction is a major consideration. On very large boats the engines and steering positions might be several yards apart and on different levels, making purely mechanical linkages practically unworkable.

Of course many of these advanced systems are impenetrable to all but the experts. If a fault develops there's not much we can do to rectify it. But for those accustomed to humbler levels of boating, it's reassuring to know that cable controls are still by far the most common.

CABLE SYSTEMS

The push-pull cable—often called a "Bowden" cable after its inventor—is really *two* cables, one inside the other. The outer casing is immobilized at both ends and the inner cable moves longitudinally to transmit a mechanical action along its length (Figure 8.1). Perhaps the most familiar application for many of us is bicycle brake cables, though the comparison isn't strictly accurate. Bicycle brake cables are only efficient when pulling, whereas the much stouter inner cables used on boats are stiff enough to push as well.

Two cables are needed on most boats, with sometimes a third to stop the engine. One operates the gearshift (clutch) and the other the throttle, being connected to cranks at the engine end and a "control head" in the cockpit. Double-lever control boxes were once standard and are still quite popular on many boat models from 30 to 60 feet. But they have since given way to more compact single-lever units on boats small enough to be propelled by stern drives and also on those large and expensive enough to easily absorb the added expense of electronic, pneumatic, or hydraulic single-lever controls.

Although not absolutely essential, it's usual to fit the control head so the lever is upright with the engine in neutral. To move ahead, the lever is pushed forward, overcoming a spring-loaded detent in the mechanism. This first action engages forward gear and, with the engine ticking over at minimum revs, the prop starts to turn. To increase the revs, the lever—now acting purely as a throttle—is pushed farther forward until you reach the desired speed.

Reverse gear and throttle is selected by following the same sequence, this time moving the gear lever aft. When in neutral, a gear disengagement button can be pressed (or on some models the entire lever is pulled away from the housing) to allow the throttle to be opened without engaging a gear.

DUAL-STATION CONTROLS

At first thought it might seem easy enough. Bring separate sets of cables down from the various steering positions, connect them to the engine, and you have multiple controls. Unfortunately, it's not that simple. Given that human disagreement can take unexpected twists, it's considered safer for the world at large if only one helmsperson at a time has control of a vessel. This means—let's say—that while the flying bridge controls are active, the ones in the wheelhouse must be disabled. If only this were always possible, and it *is* with most single-lever systems—they generally have a provision for activating only one station at a time (Figure 8.2). But considering that so many boats in the popular 30- to 60-foot range have double-lever, cable-driven sys-

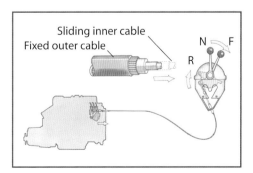

Sliding inner cable
Fixed outer cable

N   F
R

Figure 8.1   Push-pull cable system.

tems (Figure 8.3), we have to live with the reality that, on many boats, moving the control levers at one station moves them at all.

Here's how it works: the control boxes are "daisy chained" so that the upper station controls the lower station, which in turn controls the engine (and gear). Of course, it is also possible to run cables from both stations all the way to the engine compartment. But this is generally less desirable for two important and equally valid reasons. First, the increased length of cable also increases friction, which makes both sets of controls harder to operate. Equally (or perhaps more) important is the cost. Control cables are priced by the foot; daisy chaining usually saves a considerable bit of footage by using two shorter sets of cables rather than one short set and one long.

THERE ARE ALSO CABLE-BASED single-lever control units that can serve multiple stations and will only allow one station at a time to be "online." But they are complex and expensive to the degree that most U.S. builders shun them in favor of either less expensive double-lever systems or simpler, more reliable, easier-to-install (and usually no more expensive) electronic, pneumatic, or hydraulic systems.

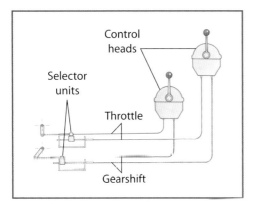

Figure 8.2   Dual-station, single-lever controls. The gear and throttle cables from both control heads go down to selector units, from which only single control outputs emerge. When both control head levers are in neutral, the first one to be operated will assume control, and the other will be inert.

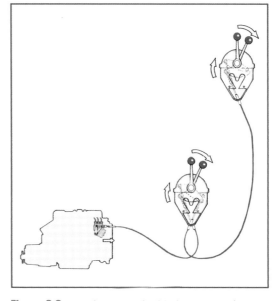

Figure 8.3   Dual-station, double-lever controls.

CHAPTER 9

Starting and Stopping Your Engine

NOW THAT YOU HAVE AN UNDERSTANDING of how your diesel engine works, along with its associated systems, it's time to put this knowledge to practical use. So let's discuss what you need to do to properly start and stop your engine(s). But it's never a good idea to simply hop aboard, start the engine and go, so we'd first better consider a thorough . . .

PRE-START CHECK

- Make sure there's nothing dangling in the water that could later foul the prop. Mooring ropes are obvious enough, but many people forget such things as fishing lines and dinghy painters.
- Check that you have enough fuel and that any shut-off valves are open.
- Check the crankcase oil level and top up if necessary.
- Also check the fresh water in the cooling system—either at the manifold or expansion tank, whichever is appropriate. And, while you're down there, have a quick look at the various belts.
- Open the raw-water inlet valve(s) (seacocks) and visually inspect the strainers for accumulated debris. Clean them before proceeding, if necessary.
- If the exhaust outlet is plugged, remove the plug. If there's a valve, make sure it's open.

STARTING

- Turn on the battery switch.
- If engine-space blowers are fitted, run these for about four minutes but turn them off to reduce battery drain before starting the engine.

- Put the gear lever in neutral, press the gear disengagement control (on most single-lever controls), and advance the throttle about one-third.
- Turn the key to the "ON" position.
- At this stage, engines with glow plug or air pre-heaters face a couple of options. Some have a button that must be depressed for 30 to 60 seconds (depending on air temperature) and then held depressed while you press the "START" button. Both buttons should be released immediately when the engine starts. Other engines have a cold-start device control as a second rotation of the switch—again holding it there long enough for it to do its job. Yet another turn of the switch (usually to the right) cranks and starts the engine. It's very important to check your manual to familiarize yourself with the correct starting procedure for your boat.

W A R N I N G

Do not crank continuously for more than 15 seconds. Starter motors can easily overheat. Crank for 15 seconds maximum, then wait 15 seconds for the motor to cool.

W A R N I N G

Prolonged cranking can flood the engine. The water pump lifts seawater into the cooling system and, without the exhaust blast to blow it clear, it can run back through the exhaust valves into the cylinders. If in doubt, close the seacock—but remember to open it as soon as the engine starts!

A FEW RUNNING CHECKS

Once the engine has started, don't put it immediately under load; go easy on the throttle. The majority of wear occurs while the engine is cold. Give it ten minutes or so to warm up and allow the oil to be distributed throughout the lubrication system. This is particularly important for turbocharged engines with their more heavily loaded bearings—not least the bearings in the turbocharger itself. In the meantime do some quick checks to determine that all is well with the engine:

- Verify that the oil pressure light and battery charge lights (and their audible alarms) have gone out. If gauges are fitted, check these instead.
- Look over the stern to make sure a decent flow of cooling water is coming out of the exhaust. Some installations have coolant temperature gauges that should gradually increase until the correct operational temperature range is reached (refer to manual for precise settings). All engines should have an audible alarm that sounds if safe levels are exceeded.

WARNING

**If there's a problem with oil pressure, charging, or cooling temperatures,
STOP THE ENGINE AT ONCE! Then do whatever is necessary to rectify the problem.**

STOPPING THE ENGINE

- Put the transmission in neutral and the throttle in the idle position.
- Allow the engine to cool for a couple of minutes or so.
- Stop the engine. But first REFER TO YOUR MANUAL. There are different ways to do this, and to get it wrong could cost you dearly. On some engines, you simply turn the key to the left as you might switch off your car. Others have a pull cable that leads to the stop control on the injection pump. Or you may have a "Stop" button (often colored red) on the engine control panel that you keep depressed until the engine stops. In the last two cases you must allow the engine to stop entirely before you turn off the key. Not doing so can seriously damage the alternator.
- If leaving the boat for any time, turn off the engine electrical supply and shut the cooling water seacock and fuel shut-off valve.

Troubleshooting Your Engine

See following pages.

THE ENGINE WON'T TURN OVER

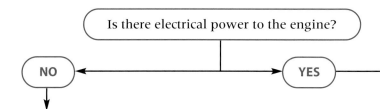

Is there electrical power to the engine?

NO ← → YES

1. Is the battery isolation switch "ON"?
2. Check for blown fuse or tripped circuit breaker.
3. Is the battery totally discharged?
4. Are the battery terminal leads connected?
5. Is the battery ground lead to the engine block connected and secure?

1. This is a common but surprisingly easy mistake to make. The usual arrangement is to have a single switch in the positive side of the circuit, but many European boats also isolate the negative side. Both must be switched on for the engine to start.

2. Engine control fuses aren't always easy to find. There may be a small fuse box mounted on the engine block somewhere or—a ridiculous practice on some engines—it could even be wound in beneath the engine wiring harness insulation! You may have to consult the service manual.

3. A battery's voltage doesn't have to be zero for it to be useless. A fully charged 12V battery at rest will show around 12.8V. By the time that reading drops to 10.5V it's effectively 100% drained. If your power management system includes a voltmeter or bar graph type state-of-charge indicator, monitoring the battery condition is very straight-

forward. If not, you will have to resort to a hydrometer or portable multi-meter.

4. Engine starting creates high electrical demands. Any voltage drop due to corroded or loose connections can result in total failure. Check that there's no corrosion and that the terminal clamps are tight on the posts.

5. The same goes for the cable that goes from the battery negative to the engine block. Vibration can easily loosen the connection, so make sure it's clean and tighten the securing bolt.

6. Starter solenoids can draw quite a lot of power. To avoid running heavy cables from the starting switch to the solenoid, a secondary switch known as a "relay" is often used. Turning the ignition key activates the relay, which, in turn, switches on the power to operate the solenoid. Relays are unserviceable items. If defective they should be replaced.

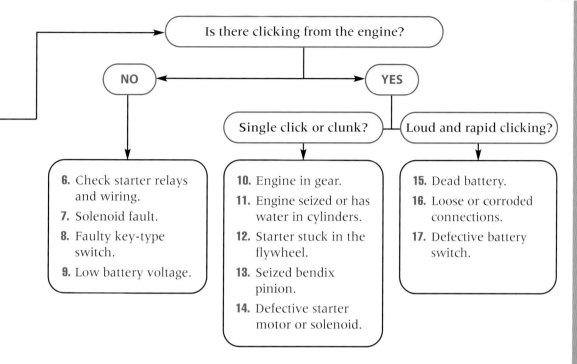

Is there clicking from the engine?

NO — YES

Single click or clunk? — Loud and rapid clicking?

6. Check starter relays and wiring.
7. Solenoid fault.
8. Faulty key-type switch.
9. Low battery voltage.

10. Engine in gear.
11. Engine seized or has water in cylinders.
12. Starter stuck in the flywheel.
13. Seized bendix pinion.
14. Defective starter motor or solenoid.

15. Dead battery.
16. Loose or corroded connections.
17. Defective battery switch.

7. Solenoids sometimes get stuck. They can often be freed by tapping them lightly with the power on. Lightly, mind you: DON'T HIT IT HARD WITH A HAMMER!

8. Key-type switches are notoriously prone to faults. Pushbuttons are much more reliable. The switch can be by-passed by connecting across the sole-noid terminals as shown on page 115.

9. If your cabin lights dim when you operate the starting switch, you can be sure the batteries are at a low state of charge. Try switching off all other appliances so the starter motor can have what little power is left.

10. Most engines will not start in gear (the shift mechanism has a switch that opens the starting circuit if the transmission isn't in neutral), so make sure the shift lever is in neutral if an engine seems totally unresponsive to the start switch.

Even if the engine will start in gear, a heavily fouled prop may cause too much resistance. Either way, it is wise to make a habit of checking that the shift lever(s) are in neutral before trying to start the engine(s).

11. If the water has only been in the engine a short time, you can act to prevent expensive damage. If the engine has seized, you are almost certainly facing a complete overhaul.

12, 13, 14. The starter motor should be removed so it can be freed up or sent away for repair.

15. If the engine can't be hand started, there's nothing for it but to find some other means of charging the battery.

16. Clean and tighten as required.

17. Bypass or replace.

THE ENGINE TURNS OVER BUT WON'T START

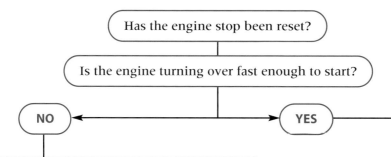

Has the engine stop been reset?

Is the engine turning over fast enough to start?

NO   YES

1. Low battery voltage.
2. Defective battery.
3. Poor electrical connections.
4. Malfunction of battery isolation switch.
5. Defective starter motor.
6. Partially seized engine or gearbox.

1, 2, 3. When it comes to engine starting, cranking speed is of the essence. Since the rotation is usually gained by electrical power, look toward the most obvious causes before suspecting anything more dramatic. Battery maintenance is covered in Chapter 12. If your batteries have deteriorated to the point that they will no longer hold their charge, there's no solution other than replacement.

However, there are a couple of tricks that might get you out of trouble. If there are decompression levers on your engine, open them until the speed mounts, then drop them down. Sailboats with manual gearboxes (not hydraulic) can allow the prop to freewheel in neutral, engaging forward gear immediately after operating the start switch.

4. Isolating switches are fairly robust by nature, but wear and sparking can damage their internal contacts, thereby increasing resistance. Replacement is the only permanent cure, but a temporary fix can be achieved by taking the switch out of the circuit entirely. The easiest way of doing this is to connect both cable terminals to the same connector post on the back of the switch.

5. The field windings could be breaking down or the bearings could be worn or partially seized. If the motor gets hot to the touch, this is a sure sign that it's drawing lots of current and ailing seriously. It should be reconditioned or replaced.

6. Time for an overhaul.

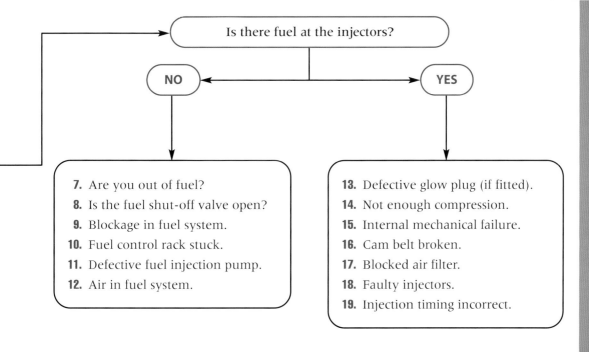

Is there fuel at the injectors?

NO   **YES**

7. Are you out of fuel?
8. Is the fuel shut-off valve open?
9. Blockage in fuel system.
10. Fuel control rack stuck.
11. Defective fuel injection pump.
12. Air in fuel system.

13. Defective glow plug (if fitted).
14. Not enough compression.
15. Internal mechanical failure.
16. Cam belt broken.
17. Blocked air filter.
18. Faulty injectors.
19. Injection timing incorrect.

7. Since tanks usually run dry while the engine is running, it would be very odd indeed if you suddenly found it empty. Check that a leak hasn't dumped the fuel into the bilge. And remember: whatever the cause, once everything is shipshape again, the system will require bleeding before you can run the engine. See Chapter 12.

8. If the valve is shut, open it.

9. The causes of blockage can be many and are covered more fully in Chapter 2. First check the pre-filter to see if there's anything in the sediment bowl. Then act accordingly.

10, 11. This is dragon country and none but the most expert should venture inside. Time to get help.

12. See Chapter 12.

13. The engine is too cold. You may have better luck at a warmer time of day or perhaps you can warm the engine gen-

tly by other means—a hot water bottle, for instance.

14. Take off the air filter and aim a couple of squirts of oil as deep into the intake manifold as possible. The objective is to allow the oil to run down the cylinder walls—it will help seal the piston rings. Be careful not to overdo it. Oil is incompressible and excessive amounts could damage the engine. As soon as the engine fires, replace the air filter. This, of course, is only a short term measure. The problem is one of general wear and tear and the need for an overhaul is imminent.

15, 16. Time to call a mechanic.

17. Replace or clean as covered in Chapter 12.

18. Replace or send away for servicing.

19. Consult your engine manual. This can be quite a simple job on some engines. If in doubt, call in a mechanic.

THE ENGINE RUNS BUT EXHIBITS ABNORMAL SYMPTOMS

Almost every engine will have some sort of warning device that gives notice that things are wrong. These might be gauges monitoring oil pressure, coolant temperature, and battery charging, or simple lights and buzzers that will be activated if worrying thresholds are exceeded. Of equal importance to these electrical guardians are the skipper's senses of sight, sound, and smell—of which the first two are by far the most important and the third the most desperate, since by then you will have missed the early signs and the engine will be seriously overheating.

SMOKE SIGNALS

A smoking exhaust can tell you a lot about the condition of the engine (Figure 10.1). Black or gray smoke is caused by unburned fuel and often contains soot that can settle to form a dirty patch on the water. Don't immediately suspect the engine —check for other causes first.

- Too much load on the engine. If black smoke emerges when moving from a standstill but clears very quickly, you may simply have opened the throttle too savagely. Or . . .
- A dirty, weed-festooned hull will cause lots of extra drag. So will towing another boat. Or . . .
- A too large or over-pitched prop. The engine is simply struggling to turn it. Or . . .
- A fouled prop. If boat speed suddenly slows this is a very likely cause. Now, to the engine . . .
- Dirty air filters. The engine simply isn't breathing deeply enough. Or . . .
- Engine space ventilation has been reduced. Look for items that might be blocking the air's path toward the engine.
- Turbo failure—again not enough air is getting into the cylinders.
- Constriction of the exhaust system is causing high back pressure. Perhaps a collapsed exhaust hose or a partially closed seacock is the problem.
- Faulty injectors or injection pump. Check everything else before you decide this is the problem. This is a job for the professionals.

Blue smoke arises from burning crankcase oil that has reached the combustion chamber, usually past worn components.

- Worn valve guides.
- Worn or seized piston rings.
- Turbo oil seal failure. Lubricating oil is escaping into the hot exhaust gases.
- Crankcase has been overfilled.

Figure 10.1   The color of the exhaust can indicate the condition of the engine.

- High crankcase pressure due to a blocked breather.
- Thermostat stuck open. The engine is running at below its normal operating temperature.

White smoke is nearly always water vapor and is quite normal when the engine is first started. However, if it persists for more than few seconds, things could be amiss with the engine.

- Water in the fuel—most probable if the engine runs erratically.
- Cracked cylinder head.
- Blown head gasket. Cooling water is escaping from the galleries and entering a combustion chamber.
- Cracked exhaust manifold.

SHAKE, RATTLE, AND ROLL

Although it's certainly possible that excessive vibration could be due to the engine itself, this is another situation in which the cause is likely to be elsewhere.

- Bent prop shaft.
- Damaged propeller. Possibly a lost blade, particularly likely with folding and feathering props. Both this and the bent shaft become prime suspects if the prop has recently been seriously fouled by flotsam.
- Broken engine mount.
- Loose shaft coupling.
- Loose shaft anode.
- Cutless bearing failure. These rarely fail catastrophically—you usually get plenty of warning.
- Gearbox failure. If so, you should be able to hear it if you can get close enough.
- Internal engine failure, such as big end bearings, main bearings, or valves. Again, this should be clearly audible.

GENERAL LACK OF PERFORMANCE

- Marine growths on hull or prop (Figure 10.2). Even a few barnacles on the propeller blades can seriously impair their efficiency as foils. The loss of drive can be very dramatic.
- Damaged prop—possibly a bent blade.
- Turbo failure or accumulated dirt.
- Blockage to the fuel system. Check the pre-filter first to make sure it's clear. You may have fallen prey to the diesel bug!

Figure 10.2 Marine growths on a propeller are one of many reasons for lack of performance.

- Cable not opening the throttle fully. It could be broken or frayed, or the holding clamp (at the engine end) could have vibrated loose.
- Engine in need of an overhaul.
- On stern drives and sail drives the propeller bushing could be slipping.

THE ENGINE HUNTS OR DIES

- Out of fuel. Either very bad planning or your fuel gauges are faulty.
- Fuel valve shut—perhaps partially.
- Blocked or partially blocked filters.
- Fuel line blocked. Suspect the diesel bug!
- Water in fuel.
- Fuel lift pump defective—perhaps a split diaphragm.
- Air in the fuel. Suspect a loose connection or leaking seal somewhere.
- Tank air vent crushed or blocked. There's a partial vacuum in the tank.
- Split fuel line.
- Fouled prop.

Possible Mechanical Causes

- Partial engine seizure due to loss of oil or serious overheating.
- Valves—perhaps a broken spring. Expect lots of noise.
- Hole in piston crown.
- Fuel injection pump problems.
- Turbo failure. There may be billows of black smoke.

OVERHEATING ALARM SOUNDS

At the earliest possible moment, reduce the revs, check the exhaust outlet for raw-water flow, and stop the engine.

If there's little or no water spurting from the exhaust the problem could be:

- Seacock partially or completely shut.
- Blocked, or partially blocked, raw-water inlet or strainer.
- Plastic bag over sail-drive leg or seacock.
- Air leak in the strainer seal—the suction is being lost and the onset of overheating is usually rapid.
- Damaged pump impeller.
- Split hose somewhere.

But if there's a good flow of water from the exhaust it could be:

- Thermostat failed in the closed position.

- Loss of freshwater coolant. This could be a hose, the heat exchanger, or maybe even a calorifier (a domestic water heater in which water is heated by the engine's freshwater coolant via heat exchange). (Be very careful when you investigate. The evidence is probably boiling hot!)
- Slack or broken drive belt. If the belt also drives the alternator, you would also expect the battery light or alarm to be activated.

OIL WARNING LIGHT OR ALARM ACTIVATED

Don't hesitate. Shut the engine down immediately. Then check for:

- Engine oil leaks.
- Crankcase oil level.
- Pressure relief valve.
- Defective sender unit or wiring.
- Big end bearing failure.
- Ruptured oil cooler.

ALTERNATOR CHARGE ALARM SOUNDS

Stop the engine and investigate. Remember the most likely cause is a broken belt, which, if it's also driving the raw-water pump, will mean the engine will rapidly overheat and the exhaust system could be seriously damaged by uncooled gases.

- Broken or slack drive belt.
- Defective alternator.
- Power to alternator field coils interrupted.
- Wiring fault or short circuit.
- Glow plug remaining on.

11

Maintaining Your Engine

IT GOES WITHOUT SAYING THAT WE must take good care of our diesel engines if they are to deliver efficient and reliable service over a number of years. But what sort of "good care" are we referring to? What exactly does it entail and at what intervals should we fulfill those tasks that will be involved?

Well, there are some pacing influences. In most parts of the world, boating is a seasonal pursuit, with alternating periods of activity and dormancy. Where boat work is concerned, these ebbs and flows make some times more convenient than others. There are also physical limitations to the useful life span of many of the substances and components—lubricating oils become contaminated, filters clog, anodes waste away, and so on. It therefore makes sense to try to match what's opportune for us with what's good for the engine.

BASIC MAINTENANCE INTERVALS

DAILY WHEN IN USE

1. Check fuel level.
2. Check crankcase oil level.
3. Check freshwater coolant level. Remember that it's extremely dangerous to open the header tank while it's still hot.
4. Conduct a general check for leakage of oil, fuel, or water.
5. Check raw-water strainer and clear if necessary.

WEEKLY WHEN IN USE

1. Check belt tensions and inspect for damage.
2. Check gearbox oil level.

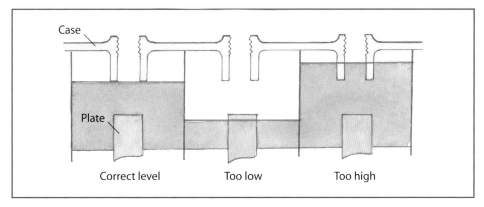

Figure 11.1   Every week, battery electrolyte levels should be checked.

3. Check for water or sediment in the fuel tank. Inspect the pre-filter bowl or drain off a sample from the bottom of the tank.

4. Check battery electrolyte levels. Top up if low (Figure 11.1).

ANNUALLY

1. Check cooling system anodes, replacing as necessary.

2. Closely inspect all hoses for cracking, bulging, or other signs of deterioration. Check all hose clips for tightness.

3. Check the air filter, wash or replace as appropriate.

4. Check the exhaust elbow for corrosion. Ideally, you should detach the exhaust so you can have a look inside.

5. Check engine mounts for deterioration. Look for loose fastenings and separation between rubber and metal components.

6. Check the shaft coupling and make sure all bolts are properly tightened.

AS RECOMMENDED BY THE ENGINE MANUFACTURER

Certain jobs relate to engine hours and can arise at any time, depending on how much the engine is used. Refer to your engine manual for the precise details, but the following are typical.

- Oil and oil filters should be changed every 100 to 150 operational hours or at the end of each season, whichever comes first.
- Gearbox oil (or transmission fluid) should also be changed every 150 hours or annually, whichever comes first.
- Replace fuel filters every 300 hours.
- It is recommended that sail-drive diaphragms should be replaced after seven years.

SCHEDULED BY THE SEASONS

The reality is that most of us shuffle our maintenance plans to fit the calendar. And there's usually no reason not to. The average sailing yacht will spend only about 50 hours per year under power, and even a motor cruiser would be pushed to make 150.

The all-important oil changes can therefore be scheduled as an annual event, and the time to start is when your boat is being put to bed for the winter. That way, the acids that are produced as a by-product of combustion won't be left to eat away at metal surfaces over the layup period. The other advantage of giving the engine a good going over in the autumn is that it leaves you plenty of time to rectify any problems you discover.

Some boats are laid up ashore while others remain afloat. It follows that jobs that might be possible in one situation won't be in the other. Do what you can.

WINTERIZING

1. Change the engine and gearbox lubrication oil, replacing any filters.
2. Drain the freshwater cooling system and refill with a fresh solution of antifreeze.
3. Flush the raw-water system with fresh water if possible, then run enough antifreeze through the system to ensure there is no trapped fresh water.
4. Check the raw-water filter. Clean if necessary.
5. Remove the pump impeller. Pop it into a plastic bag and tie it to the keys so you won't forget to refit it!
6. Drain any water or sediment from the fuel tank and fill the tank if possible.
7. Also drain any contaminants from the pre-filter. Replace the filter element.
8. If possible, squirt a little oil into the air intake and turn over the engine (don't start it!) to distribute it over the cylinder walls. Some manufacturers recommend removing the injectors and introducing the oil that way—refitting the injectors once you have done so. Always follow manufacturer's recommendations to the letter.
9. Change the air filter and stuff an oily rag into the intake. Do the same to the exhaust. Then hang a notice on the engine to remind yourself they are there!
10. Relax or remove all belts. If the former, relax them enough to be obvious.
11. Rinse out the antisiphon valve with fresh water. Reassemble if you've taken it apart.
12. Check the engine over thoroughly. Your inspection should include: the engine mounts, hoses and their clamps, exhaust and the exhaust elbow, and the electrical wiring. If there's something amiss, this is the time to know about it.
13. Remove the batteries and charge them fully. If the boat is to be wintered afloat, clean the terminals and protect them with petroleum jelly. Wherever they are, recharge them every month or so.

ONCE SPRING HAS SPRUNG

1. Check freshwater coolant and top up if necessary.
2. Check oil levels and top up if necessary.
3. Refit pump impeller.
4. Unseal any openings you might have plugged in the autumn.
5. Retighten all belts.
6. Reconnect batteries.
7. Check stern gland lubrication. Give the remote greaser a couple of turns.
8. Start the engine as recommended in Chapter 9.
9. Enjoy!

TOOLS

It seems a central truth that no matter how many tools you carry, one day you will come across a problem that calls for some implement you haven't got. Since it's in the very nature of boats to venture to places where outside assistance is scarce, a wise skipper will prepare for the day when she may have to roll up her sleeves and get herself out of trouble. Of course you can't anticipate every event, but at least you can ensure that most contingencies are covered (Figure 11.2).

Buy the best tools you can afford. The inexperienced mechanic needs all the help he can get, and certainly can do without the deficiencies of cheap and nasty gear. Wrenches that don't fit well can round off nuts and bolt heads. The very cheapest may be cast, rather than forged, which means they are much weaker and

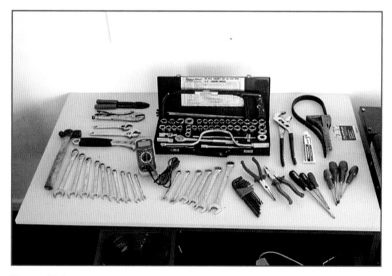

Figure 11.2   Every boat should carry a good selection of high-quality tools.

could break—often with disastrous consequences to your knuckles. Screwdrivers with soft tips can damage the slots on screws. Compared to the value of the equipment you'll be working on, the cost of a really good tool is trifling.

European, Japanese, and modern British engines almost invariably have metric bolts and fastenings, while those made in America may well be using imperial. But, when assembling your own toolkit, don't forget the rest of the boat. Although this book is concerned with diesel engines and their associated gear, most boats are bristling with other mechanical paraphernalia that might one day require attention. Across the whole gamut, you may well find a wide mix of fastening types on board.

MECHANICAL TOOLKIT

- **Workshop manual.** The owner's manual that comes with the engine is rarely sufficient. The real thing should cost less than an average takeout meal and is worth every penny.
- **Wrenches.** 7 mm to 24 mm in metric sizes; 1/4 in. to 1 in. in imperial. Combination wrenches have open jaws on one end and full-circle "box ends" on the other—both fitting the same size nuts. Wrenches with open jaws at both ends are sized differently—i.e., 12 mm and 14 mm—meaning you only need half the number to cover the whole range. Since you often need a pair of wrenches of the same size for some jobs, it makes sense to carry a set of both combination and open-jawed wrenches.
- **Adjustable wrenches.** These might make a professional cringe but there's no doubt they come in handy—particularly in larger sizes, when they can really be effective. Choose one with jaws that open wider than your largest wrench size and a smaller one for more general use.
- **Socket set.** Either 3/8 in. or 1/2 in. drive. The former is the most handy in restricted spaces but is not always hefty enough with larger sockets. Ideally you should carry both, and even the tiny 1/4 in. drive sets are useful. Many sets include sockets for both metric and imperial bolts; if not, buy one set of each.
- **Strap wrench.** For removing filter elements. Absolutely essential.
- **Screwdrivers.** A comprehensive selection including flat-bladed and cross-point (Phillips and/or Posidrive) in a range of sizes. The short "stubby" types are very handy where space is tight.
- **Pliers.** Conventional and needle-nose. Also very useful are what are known as "water pump pliers" or "Channellocks," which can be opened to grip large objects. Unless in the direst circumstances, never use pliers for gripping nuts or bolt heads. You will almost certainly cause permanent damage.
- **Locking pliers**, e.g., "Vise-Grips"—another tool that will bring a shudder to all sensitive souls, but far too versatile and useful not to be included.
- **Hacksaw and spare blades.**
- **Craft knife and spare blades.**

- **Set of Allen wrenches.** Yet another choice to be made between metric and imperial, but make sure they're good and long because you often need the leverage.
- **Hammer.** Two types are useful: the ball peen "mechanic's" hammer and those with a hard rubber or plastic head. Ball peen hammers should be fairly light in weight, if only to spare the engine, while the soft-headed type can be as heavy as is reasonable.
- **Feeler gauges**—again metric or imperial. You might use these to check prop shaft alignment or to adjust the tappets.
- **Punches.** Parallel or "straight" type. For driving out obstinate "roll" or "cotter" pins—and, of course, the occasional obstinate bolt. A range of sizes would be ideal, say between 3 mm and 8 mm.
- **Magnet** for recovering dropped components from the bilge.
- **Oil change pump**—assuming your engine doesn't have one built in. These will pull the crankcase oil up through the dipstick pipe, which is the only practical method on many boats. The pumps may be of a simple piston type or have a reservoir in which a partial vacuum is formed, containing the waste oil as it's extracted.
- **Grease gun** and **small squirt-type oil can.**

ELECTRICAL TOOLKIT

- **Multimeter**—preferably the digital type that is easier to read with your head down in the engine bay.
- **Wire strippers** and **crimpers**, either as separate implements or a multipurpose tool.
- **Test light**—often sold with a small screwdriver as a probe.
- **Hydrometer** for testing battery charge—only appropriate if your batteries are liquid lead-acid type with accessible cells. If not, you will have to rely on your multimeter.

SPARES

- **Oil** for engine and gearbox.
- **Oil filter.**
- **Fuel filters**—at least one spare element or cartridge for each.
- **Air cleaner element**, if appropriate.
- **Crankcase breather elements**, if fitted.
- **Various greases** for pumps, stern glands, and general use.
- **Penetrating oil** in an aerosol can.
- **Pump impellers**—particularly for the raw-water-cooling pump. If going any distance, carry at least a couple.
- **Thermostat.** Some engines have more than one, so check the manual.

- **Antifreeze**—sufficient for a complete freshwater-cooling circuit change.
- **Belts**—at least one spare of each.
- **Hoses.**
- **Anodes.** Raw-water-cooled engines have them fitted in their blocks, but you will also find them in oil coolers and other heat exchangers. Regular replacement is imperative.
- **Gasket material and sealant.**
- **PTFE** (e.g., Teflon) tape.

ELECTRICAL SPARES

- **Spare crimp-type connectors** in a variety of sizes.
- **Fuses.**
- **Deionized** (or distilled) water for battery top-up (if appropriate).
- **Insulating tape.**
- **Heat-shrink tape.**
- **Petroleum jelly** (Vaseline).

CHAPTER 12

Critical Procedures and How to Do Them

TAKE CARE OF YOUR FUEL FILTERS

As we discussed in Chapter 2, the ideal arrangement is to have the fuel supply run the gauntlet of a pair of filters before it reaches the engine. The first is called the pre-filter (or primary filter) and is usually fitted remotely from the engine, somewhere accessible in the run of the fuel line. The second is known as the fine filter (or secondary filter) and is invariably mounted on the engine assembly. Although they aren't identical, there are similarities, both in their construction and in the way you maintain them.

You should check your engine manual, but replacement intervals of 200 to 300 engine hours are typical. If your fuel becomes contaminated the pre-filter will need more frequent replacement—in severe cases down to a matter of minutes!

Even if everything seems to be working well, don't be tempted to stretch the replacement schedule. The fuel might look clear, but tiny particles will have been building up in the filter elements since the very first drop passed through them—and then there are those asphaltenes we came across in Chapter 2.

There are three distinct types of filters:

1. Replaceable element: such as Racor and Separ (Figure 12.1)
2. Cartridge: such as CAV (Figure 12.2)
3. Spin-on: such as Fleetguard (Figure 12.3)

Pre-filters often (and ideally) have a watertrap at the bottom of the filter. Let's start there.

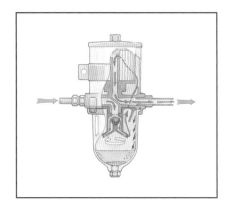

Figure 12.1   Replaceable filter.

Figure 12.2   Cartridge-type filter.

Figure 12.3   Spin-on filter.

DRAINING A WATERTRAP

If your pre-filter has a transparent bowl, any water or sediment trapped in it should be clearly visible. The bowls on some filters are metal (or metal-shielded) and must be drained to see what they contain. Though a small valve or petcock might seem more convenient for ease of draining (and some older filters are fitted this way), current Coast Guard regulations require a tapered pipe plug.

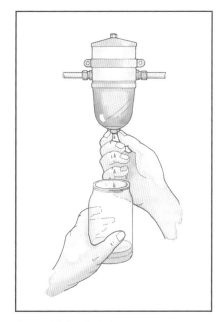

1. Place a suitable container underneath, before loosening the plug (Figure 12.4).
2. Once the fuel is running clear, screw the plug shut. Don't overtighten the plug. It's hollow and easily damaged. Some are plastic, and their threads are fragile.

No air should have entered the system, so it won't need bleeding.

Figure 12.4   Draining a watertrap.

REPLACING FILTER ELEMENTS

Before you disassemble any filter lying below the level in the fuel tank, it's important to close the fuel valve. If you don't, you'll have an almighty mess on your hands as the tank attempts to empty itself into the bilge. If you are fortunate enough or have had the foresight to fit parallel filters (see Chapter 2), make sure the selector valve is turned away from the filter you are working on. Spillage will be limited and less air will enter the system.

Replaceable elements come in a variety of sizes to fit different capacity filter/water separators; be sure to use the proper size for your unit (Figure 12.5).

Working tidily is important. Diesel fuel is invasive stuff and the better it is contained the happier you will be. Hang a plastic bag (trash bin liners work well) or put a bowl beneath the filter to catch the drips. And scatter some rags around to absorb any splatters.

Clean off any external dirt before you go any further. You don't want it to find its way into the body of the filter as you work.

ALWAYS DISABLE THE ENGINE, either by removing the key from the start switch or by disconnecting the battery. You don't want anyone firing it up while you're working on it!

CARTRIDGE-TYPE FILTERS

With these the filter element is contained in a metal cylinder clamped between the filter head and a base plate. A frequent addition to the basic unit is either a glass or metal bowl fitted immediately below the cartridge. The whole assembly is held together by a bolt running down from the top of the unit.

1. Ensure the plastic bag (or other container) is in place. You are about to release the contents of the filter into it.
2. Unscrew the center bolt. The three main components will separate and the fuel will drain into the bag.
3. Pull off the old canister and check the sealing rings. It's not absolutely necessary to replace the upper seal every time but, since new seals come with the new filter, you may prefer to anyway. If the filter has a glass or metal bowl, the seal between the bowl and the cartridge should always be changed, since it has probably stretched.

Figure 12.5   Replaceable filter elements. (Courtesy Racor)

4. To put it all back together, simply reverse the procedure. The best way is to assemble the base plate, bowl, and cartridge with all their seals in place and offer it up to the filter head as a single stack. Make sure everything has gone back in the correct order and is properly seated.

5. While holding the stack in place, insert the bolt and hand tighten—quite a fiddly job. Finally, tighten the bolt firmly but not too savagely with a wrench.

Many filters of this type have a removable screw plug in the head casting that allows you to top them up them with fuel before bleeding the remaining small air bubbles from the system. See Chapter 2.

REPLACEABLE-ELEMENT FILTERS

These are normally found on larger engines. Access to the elements is through a removable lid on the top—either secured with a central T-handle bolt or four small screws.

1. First open the drain and take a small sample of fuel. If the fuel is clear you won't have to empty the whole bowl, which makes life easier.

2. Undo the T-handle bolt or screws and lift off the lid. The fuel level should be close to the top.

3. Slowly lift out the old element, avoiding spillage as much as possible. Some filters of this type will have a sprung plastic cage that must be taken out first. Make a careful note of which way up it goes.

4. Equally slowly insert the new element into the filter housing. It will absorb fuel as it becomes immersed. If there is a cage, replace that as well.

5. Check the lid's sealing ring or gasket and the O-ring under the T-handle (if there is one). Fit a new one if in any doubt.

6. Replace the lid and secure.

If this operation is done carefully you shouldn't need to bleed the system at all. But if it had been necessary to drain the unit because of contaminants, or if there had been any other significant spillage, it's possible to refill the filter from a small can before refitting the lid—again, averting the need to bleed.

SPIN-ON FILTERS

See Changing the Oil and Filter on page 100. The changing procedure is effectively the same as for spin-on oil filters.

The fuel system must be bled after the change.

BLEEDING THE FUEL SYSTEM

For the engine to run properly—if at all—the fuel that reaches the injection system must be free of air. Air can enter by various means—running out of fuel or the replacement or servicing of components are typical causes. Although some engines are self-bleeding—i.e., will purge the air unassisted—most require outside intervention.

The process of bleeding involves filling the system with fuel along its path from tank to engine, and allowing the air to escape at various points. Manual operation of the fuel lift pump is the most common method of propelling the fuel through the system while you do this, but some engines have a dedicated pump fitted elsewhere—perhaps on the fuel filter housing or injection pump. If ever there was a time to consult your engine manual, this is it.

Arm yourself with a means of mopping up as you work—rags or paper towels are useful here. Diesel fuel can attack the insulation on electrical wiring, so you don't want it sprayed over the engine.

1. Make sure the tank has plenty of fuel in it and that its shut-off valve is open.
2. Try the lift pump's operating handle to see if it's working fully. If there's little or no stroke, it's due to the position of the drive cam inside the engine. Give the engine half a turn and try again.
3. If the pre-filter is below the fuel level in the tank, and the fuel is drawn directly from the bottom of the tank—that's to say, not through a dip pipe outlet—all you have to do is crack open the bleed screw on the top of the pre-filter and it will fill itself by gravity. If not, keep the screw closed and turn your attention to the fine filter.
4. Open the bleed screw on the fine filter and start operating the lever on the fuel lift pump. Don't be surprised if this takes several minutes. Depending on how successfully you filled the pre-filter and how much drain-back has occurred in the fuel lines, there could be a fair bit of air in the system. First, you should start to see fuel fill the pre-filter bowl (assuming there is one) and then it will start emerging from the fine filter's bleed screw. Once the latter is free of bubbles or froth, pinch up the bleed screw to seal it.

This should be enough for some engines. But not the Yanmar GM series, Perkins, Thornycroft, and those based on Kubota.

1. For them, the next stage is the injection pump. Remember, you are still on the low-pressure side of the system, so undo the bleed screw and return to your labors on the lift pump. When clear fuel emerges, tighten the bleed screw.
2. Some older rotary injection pumps have a pair of bleed screws. You will need to do them both, starting with the lower of the two.
3. Give the lift pump a few more strokes for good measure.

This really should be enough. Try starting the engine in the normal way. If it runs smoothly, congratulate yourself on a job well done. If not, stop the engine but leave the key in the ignition. The final stage is on the high-pressure side of the system—beyond the puny capabilities of the lift pump.

1. Loosen all the injection pipe nuts at the injectors about a couple of turns.
2. Set the throttle to full ahead, out of gear.

3. Turn the engine over using the ignition key. Limit yourself to bursts of no more than 15 seconds to avoid burning out the starter motor. It isn't designed for continuous running.

4. First you should see air bubbles around the nuts, which will then become spurts of fuel. Once satisfied that there's no more air, tighten the injector nuts.

5. Start the engine.

WARNING

The pressure of the fuel emerging from the injection pipes is enough to drive it through your skin. Keep your fingers away from the nuts while the engine is turning over.

TIP: Paint all bleed points a conspicuous color to help identify them.

CHANGING THE OIL AND FILTER

It can't be overemphasized how important it is to maintain the quality of the lubricating oil. And don't judge it by its color. That dark gray glop that emerges on the end of your dipstick is no cause for panic. The oil got that way within hours of being poured into the engine. The change in color is simply due to detergents and combustion by-products and is entirely normal.

The best way to know that your engine oil is in good condition is to follow the replacement schedule recommended by the manufacturer. Some manufacturers recommend an oil change every 150 engine hours or at the end of each season (whichever comes first) with a fresh filter every 300 hours—i.e., every second oil change. But many mechanics claim that, in view of their relatively low cost, it makes more sense to replace the filter every time you change the oil. That way, there's no danger of forgetting where you are in the schedule and the two jobs can be regarded as one.

As with the fuel filters, arm yourself with plastic bags and rags—and a pair of rubber gloves, since this is messy work. Also, consult your engine manual to establish both the correct grade of oil and the quantity needed.

EXTRACTING THE OLD OIL

1. Run the engine for 10 to 15 minutes, preferably in gear, to bring it up to its normal operating temperature. This will thin the oil and stir any sludge in the sump into suspension.

2. Extract the oil. Some engines can be drained by removing a sump plug. More often, the oil must be pumped out, either by way of a pre-fitted pump, or out through the dipstick tube. A piston-type pump with a thin plastic tube capable of reaching the bottom of the sump can be used, but the easiest and cleanest way is to use a vacuum-type extractor that draws the oil into its own container (Figure 12.6). When buying such an extractor, make sure it has the capacity to hold all the oil in one go.
3. Be careful. Remember the oil is very hot.

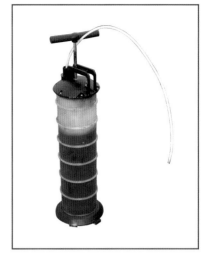

Figure 12.6 Extracting sump oil with a vacuum-type extractor.

REPLACING THE FILTER

These are usually of the spin-on type, but larger engines may have cartridge filters (without drain bowls), in which case you should refer back to the beginning of this chapter.

1. Use a filter wrench to unscrew the filter until it's just hand tight—that's to say, before any oil leaks out.
2. Place a plastic bag around the filter and continue to undo it while oil drains into the bag. As soon as it comes free, put the bag and filter safely in a bucket.
3. Remove any packaging from the new filter and check that the seals are in place.
4. Smear oil around the seal and screw on the replacement, being careful not to cross-thread it. Do it up as tightly as possible by hand. If you're strong enough, this might be enough. If not, tighten it with the wrench but don't *over*tighten it—you may be the unfortunate person who has to take it off next time!

REFILL THE OIL

Check your engine manual to determine the grade and quantity of oil required. Since you probably haven't got every drop of old oil out of the sump, you may find you need a little less.

1. Open the oil filler and wipe away any dirt before arranging a rag around it to confine spillage.
2. Pour in the oil, slowing as you approach the recommended amount. Check the dipstick frequently after allowing the oil time to work its way down to the crankcase (Figure 12.7).

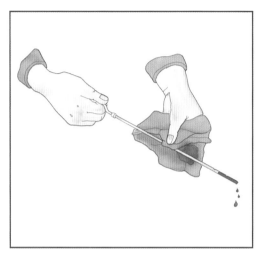

Figure 12.7   Refill until the oil level settles between the two marks. Don't forget to allow time for it to drain all the way to the sump.

CHANGING GEARBOX OIL

Since there are no combustion by-products, the oil in the gearbox should remain clean. If the oil has turned black, there may be a problem: the oil could be over-heating due to a faulty clutch. If the oil has emul-sified—i.e., turned a milky color—it could be that seawater is leaking in through the oil cooler. If that's the case, don't run the engine. Get it checked by a mechanic.

But, let's assume everything looks normal.

Gather together the usual mopping-up imple-ments and check in your manual for the type and quantity of the oil. Some gearboxes take the same oil as the engine; others use automatic transmis-sion fluid (ATF).

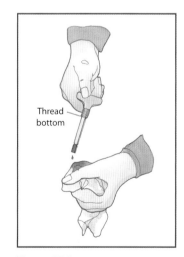

Thread bottom

Figure 12.8   Don't screw the dipstick in when checking the gearbox oil level. Measure from the bottom of the thread.

1. Remove the dipstick.
2. Extract the old oil, using the same pump as for the engine.
3. Pour in the new oil, checking the level with the dipstick. It's usual not to screw the dip-stick in when you do this. The correct reading is from the bottom of the thread (Figure 12.8).
4. When satisfied, replace the dipstick and nip it up tight.

CHANGING OR ADJUSTING THE ALTERNATOR BELT

Reinforced rubber belts are an effective way of transmitting power from one part of the engine to another. They are used for a variety of purposes—the most common being to spin the alternator. Often, a single belt will be called on to perform more than one task, perhaps driving the raw-water pump as well. And, since their workings are entirely external, they are exceptionally easy to inspect and maintain. In short, there are few excuses for allowing them to deteriorate to the point of failure.

The most common type of belt on smaller engines is trapezoidal in section—shaped like an equilateral triangle with the point cut off. These are called V-belts, and they run in pulleys having tapered grooves. The belts are tensioned so they wedge into the grooves, thereby receiving the grip that prevents them from slipping.

Larger engines will probably have flat (sometimes called *serpentine*) belts, which are both wider and thinner than V-belts.

If belts are tensioned too much, they will impart side loads on the pulleys. This will lead to accelerated wear to their bearings. If the tension is too loose, there won't be enough grip and the belt will slip and the rubber will be worn away. If you see deposits of black dust anywhere in the region, it's a sure sign of belt wear.

The object, therefore, is to get the tension exactly right—fortunately an easy trick to master. To check a V-belt's tension, press on its longest span. You should be able to deflect it about 10 to 12 mm (approximately half an inch). The way to test a flat belt is to grip it between thumb and forefinger and try to twist it through 90°. If it twists too easily, the belt is too slack (Figure 12.9).

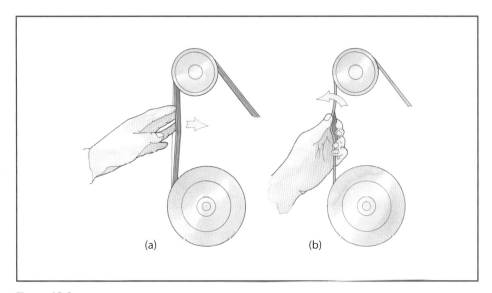

Figure 12.9 Changing or adjusting the alternator belt. (a) A V-belt's tension should allow you to deflect it by about one-half inch. (b) When correctly tensioned it should just be possible to twist a flat belt through 90°.

While you're about it, look for fraying or other problems. Remember that if an alternator belt fails, battery charging ceases. More seriously, if the belt also drives the raw-water pump, the flow stops and the engine could overheat and seize. If in doubt (see Chapter 4), replace the belt immediately—a job that should take no more than a couple of minutes.

Let's assume the belt tension is too slack and you want to tighten it. Belt tension is adjusted by moving the alternator either toward or away from the engine. The alternator pivots on a supporting bracket and is braced with a slotted (and often curved) strut clamped into place with an adjustment bolt.

1. To relax the tension, slacken—but don't remove—the bolts securing the alternator, including the one on the engine end of the slotted strut.
2. If the belt is damaged and you've decided to replace it, first remove the old one. Pivot the alternator in as far as it will go toward the engine and roll the belt out of the groove. Take time to inspect and clean the pulleys—particularly of any rust (which is abrasive) or grease (slippery).
3. Now fit the new belt, first over the flywheel pulley then over any others, leaving the alternator till last. You may find it helps to slowly rotate the flywheel by hand while easing that final bight over the rim and into its groove.
4. The alternator must be pulled away from the engine to re-tension the belt, and this is best achieved using a short length of wood—try a hammer handle—to give you a bit of leverage. Wedge your lever between the engine block and the alternator and pull outward. Tighten the various bolts, starting with the ones on the strut.
5. Check the tension as before, and again after two or three hours of running. A new belt may stretch a little.

ADJUSTING A PACKED GLAND

As described in Chapter 7, this type of stern gland relies for its watertightness on the compression of a braided packing material. The packing comes pre-impregnated with a lubricant—traditionally tallow—and then is either smeared with grease on assembly or has an external screw cup or remote greaser to dispense more grease from time to time—every four to six hours being typical.

Stuffing boxes are intended to leak a little—one to five drips a minute is about right. The adjustment is critical: too loose and your bilges will fill; too tight and wear to both the gland packing and shaft will be rapid. In extreme cases, friction could even wrench the gland from the stern tube, whereupon you will find large quantities of water all too eager to come aboard.

Assuming the stuffing box was set up correctly in the first place, it can only become looser with wear. The first signs may be an increase in the drip rate, but this can be masked by squeezing in more grease. A more reliable indication is the remote greaser itself. As the packing wears away, the contact between the shaft and the packing gets slacker, and the task of screwing down the handle becomes easier. To confirm your suspicions check the following. If anything more than traces of grease are exuding from the stuffing box, the gland needs adjustment.

1. With the engine stopped and out of gear, wipe away any excess grease and rotate the shaft by hand. It probably turns too freely—though this is a matter of judgment and difficult to define.
2. After backing off any locknuts, tighten the adjustment screws (or threaded collar) a fraction of a turn—equally, of course, since the compression must be even. It's advisable to proceed in small increments, so you don't have to ease off later.
3. Try turning the shaft again. There should be some resistance, but not a lot. Remember, better too little than too much. Count the drips: anywhere between one and five per minute will do fine.
4. When you think you've got it right, tighten any locknuts and run the engine in gear for ten minutes or so. Then go below and feel the stuffing box. It should be quite cool to the touch. If it is hot, it has been overtightened and must be slackened a little.

ALTHOUGH NOT IDEAL, stuffing boxes are often adjusted with the boat ashore, where, of course, there will be no telltale drips to guide you. This means you must judge by the rotational resistance of the shaft alone. Squirt some liquid dish detergent (or boat cleaning liquid such as Boat Zoap) into the cutless bearing to prevent any friction there from deceiving you.

REPACKING A STERN GLAND

There comes a point when no amount of adjustment will do, and you must face the fact that the gland packing needs replacing. This is a job that, for obvious reasons, should never be attempted afloat!

Here's how.

1. Remove the adjustment screws or collar from the stuffing box and slide the compressor part up the prop shaft.
2. The next stage is fiddly. The old packing has to be hoicked out of its recess. A good trick is to use a woodscrew—preferably a brass one to avoid scratching the shaft—that you screw into the packing, then pull out with pliers. A small bradawl and bits of bent wire might also come in handy. Make sure that all of the packing is removed.
3. Measure the gap between the shaft and the inside of the casing. This will indicate the size (meaning thickness) of the packing you will need. These measurements could well be in imperial units—i.e., fractions of an inch—though

(a)

(b)

Figure 12.10   Wrap the new packing around the shaft and make a single cut (a). The result will be a number of "rings" that will fit exactly (b).

new packing material may be sold in equivalent metric sizes. For example a 6.5 mm packing would replace one of 1/4 in. The length of each piece, of course, will equal the circumference of the shaft.

4. To cut the new packing to size, wrap it around the prop shaft the appropriate number of times, making sure there are no twists in it. Then take a very sharp knife and slice lengthwise along the coil so the packing is cut into individual pieces (Figure 12.10). You don't need to crawl into the engine space to do this. Choose an easily accessible bit of the shaft—even outside the boat if it's ashore.

5. Smear each piece of packing with grease, curl them around the shaft and tamp them into the recess, ensuring they sit squarely on the shaft and that their cut ends don't coincide. If there are four rings in total, you may find it helpful to temporarily assemble and tighten down the compressor tube and its securing mechanism after the third ring. This will consolidate the packing and make room for the last one.

6. Reassemble the stuffing box and rotate the shaft several times to help the packing bed down. It should turn freely. The final adjustment is best left until the boat is afloat. Hang a very conspicuous sign somewhere to remind yourself!

CHANGING A THERMOSTAT

Thermostats (see Chapter 4) are not items that need servicing. They either work or they don't. When they fail, they must be replaced. Locate the thermostat housing and remove the bolts. Lift out the old thermostat and discard it if it fails the test (see below)—or simply fit a new one to be on the safe side. Reverse the procedure to reassemble.

If the engine overheats and water still spurts from the exhaust, it's a fair bet that the thermostat has failed in the closed position. However, if you find blue smoke coming from the exhaust, there's a possibility that the engine is running too cool because the thermostat is stuck open. The first situation is the most common and demands immediate attention. Thermostats only rarely fail when open. If they do, you can be rather more relaxed about when you deal with it.

Removing a thermostat is a fairly simple matter (Figure 12.11).

1. Identify the housing—typically dome shaped and close to the forward end of the cylinder head.
2. The top of the housing is usually held down with a couple of bolts. Undo them.
3. Lift out the old thermostat and replace it with a new one. Alternatively, test the old one as described in the next section. If it's still working properly you may want to continue using it.
4. Reassemble, making sure that all gaskets go back as before.

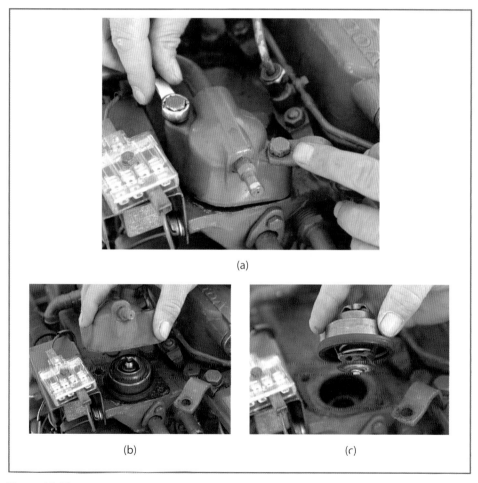

(a)

(b)   (c)

Figure 12.11 Changing a thermostat. (a) Locate the thermostat housing and remove the bolts. (b) Lift out the old thermostat and discard it. (c) Replace it with a new one.

TESTING A THERMOSTAT

If the valve is jammed open when you remove it, you will know immediately that it's defective. If it's closed you can perform a simple test to see whether it's working or not.

Immerse the thermostat in a saucepan of water and heat it on the galley stove. It should start to open at around 75°C to 85°C (167°F to 185°F)—a range well short of the boiling point. If the water boils and the valve stays shut, it's clearly faulty.

RENEWING THE FRESHWATER COOLANT

The role of antifreeze is broader than the term would suggest. As well as guarding against frost damage, almost all antifreeze contains rust and corrosion inhibitors that help protect the system. The effectiveness of these additives declines with time, so the coolant should be replaced every year, regardless of whether or not there's a risk of freezing.

1. Remove the pressure cap from the filler.
2. Locate the drain cocks—there's often more than one. Place a bowl underneath and open the cocks one by one until they run dry. Don't drain the coolant into the bilge and pump it out later. Ethylene glycol antifreeze is very toxic (propylene glycol is much safer but, unfortunately, more expensive, which discourages its use).
3. Once the system is empty, close the seacocks. The proportion of antifreeze to water depends on the lowest temperature that might occur in your area. There should be details of recommended mix ratios with the antifreeze. Err on the generous side if you want. In fact, a 50-50 mixture often provides superior heat transfer and anticorrosion protection and thus may be advisable even when not absolutely necessary for protection against freezing. Your engine manual will tell you the total capacity of the system, so it's a fairly easy matter to work out how much of the final mix you will need.
4. Pour the antifreeze into the engine first, then top up with water.
5. Run the engine for about 30 minutes to mix the two together.
6. Check the coolant level again once it has cooled down. Top up again as necessary.

WARNING

Never remove the filler cap while the engine is hot. Remember, the coolant is under pressure and serious scalds can be caused by steam and water bursting out.

REPLACING THE RAW-WATER PUMP IMPELLER

This could either be a routine check or because the raw-water flow has stopped. In the latter case the engine is overheating and you will doubtless have shut it down. You've checked the cooling water inlet strainer and it's clear of obstructions. The next most obvious culprit is the raw-water pump—or, more specifically, the rubber impeller it contains.

1. Undo the screws and remove the pump's faceplate.
2. The impeller might look intact, but it pays to take a closer look to be sure. Grip one of its vanes with a pair of needle-nose pliers and pull it out. Alternatively—or if all the vanes are missing—use a pair of screwdrivers to lever it out (Figure 12.12). Be careful to avoid damaging the edges of the brass casting. It helps to wrap the screwdriver shanks in masking tape to cushion them.
3. With the impeller extracted, examine it closely—particularly the vane roots. If you find any cracks, discard it.
4. If there are vanes missing, they have to have gone somewhere. They might have been pumped upward toward the heat exchanger but, equally, they could have dropped back into the suction tube. Whatever it takes, hunt them down until they are all accounted for. Drawing them through a new impeller could undo all your good work.
5. Clean all traces of the old paper gasket from the face of the housing.
6. Smear the new impeller lightly with dish detergent or other liquid cleaner, such as hand soap, Boat Zoap, or other wash-down detergent and slide it back

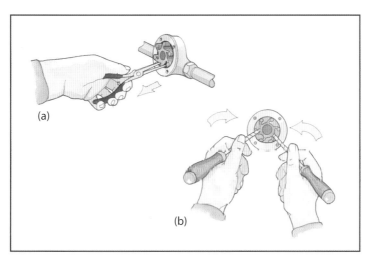

(a)

(b)

Figure 12.12 Replacement of the raw-water pump impeller.
(a) Needle-nose pliers can be used to remove the impeller . . .
(b) or you can use a pair of screwdrivers.

onto its shaft, making sure the pin (or grub screw) engages properly with the slot and that the vanes trail backward from the direction of rotation.

7. Fit a new gasket and replace the faceplate. Tighten the screws evenly in rotation.

ADJUSTING VALVE CLEARANCE

This is a task that comes round every 600 engine hours or so. Compared to other routine maintenance, it may seem fairly daunting, but it really is very simple. Consult your engine manual before attempting this job (Figure 12.13).

On most engines the opening and closing of the intake and exhaust valves is controlled by a camshaft deep in the engine. The cams lift pushrods that rise upward into the cylinder head, and these in turn operate the rocker arms that actually depress—and thereby open—the valves.

Because the various components expand as the engine gets hot, it's necessary to have a small gap between the rocker arms and valve stems. This gap is known as the *valve clearance*. The precise size of that clearance will be specified in your engine manual—somewhere in the region of 0.2 mm (0.0079 in.) is typical for a mid-size sailboat auxiliary.

Each valve clearance will be at its maximum when the cam that controls it is imparting zero lift—i.e., its lobe will be 180° from the pushrod.

Since we can't see the cam, we must deduce the position of its lobe from the actions of the rocker arms.

1. Obtain the correct valve clearances from your engine manual, and establish whether the adjustments should be made with the engine hot or cold.

2. Remove the rocker cover, exposing the rocker arms and valve stems.

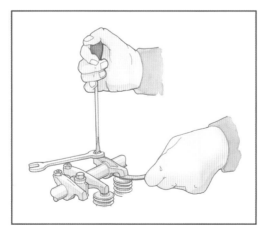

Figure 12.13   Adjusting valve clearance. Consult your engine manual before attempting this job.

3. Rotate the engine by hand in the direction it normally turns. If necessary, use a large wrench on the crankshaft nut (the big one in the center of the flywheel).

4. For now let's assume a single-cylinder engine. When one valve is fully depressed, the other is ready for adjustment.

5. Slacken the locknut on the rocker arm's adjustment screw and unscrew the screw itself a couple of turns.

6. Select the appropriate blade from your feeler gauge and slip it into the gap between the top of the valve stem and the rocker arm.

7. Turn the screw to close the gap so it just grips the feeler gauge. The grip should be positive but still light enough to be able to pull the feeler gauge out without a struggle. But not yet!

8. With the feeler gauge in place, hold the adjustment screw in position with a screwdriver while tightening the locknut. Give the gauge a little wiggle to check that nothing has moved and slide it out.

9. Turn the engine by hand so the valve you have just done is fully depressed and then adjust the other valve in the same manner.

10. On a multicylindered engine you simply repeat the procedure with each cylinder in turn. Admittedly, this is a somewhat laborious process. Experienced mechanics bring each cylinder to the top of its compression stroke (see Chapter 1) when both valves are closed and adjust their clearances. However, since this isn't a job you will need to do every day, the time-consuming but less confusing method is probably the safest way to go.

BATTERY MAINTENANCE

If treated kindly, batteries will deliver years of service. If abused, expect them to fail in double-quick time (Figure 12.14). There's a limit to what we can do, but even modest attention will extend their lives.

- Keep the batteries as fully charged as possible. This is rarely a problem with marina-based boats where shore power is available. Boats kept on moorings should consider solar panels. Even a small panel will stem the natural process of self-discharge.
- With liquid (wet-cell) lead-acid batteries, it's vital to keep the electrolyte level topped up. Check them regularly. Fill each cell to the bottom of the filler neck with distilled or deionized water.
- Keep all connections clean and free of corrosion deposits. Remove the cable clamps from the terminal posts and wash the posts with a solution of baking soda and water before brightening them up with a wire brush or small piece of emery paper.
- Smear the posts with a light film of petroleum jelly (Vaseline) immediately before refitting the cable clamps. Then apply some more over the whole connection to keep moisture at bay.

Figure 12.14 Examples of marine batteries.

Figure 12.15   Compare the corroded pencil zinc anode (right) with a brand-new one (left). Note that the only visible portion of an installed zinc is the outer end of the brass plug, which means that the state of the zinc itself will be totally unknown until you remove it. (Courtesy Canada Metals)

REPLACING ENGINE ANODES

All raw-water-cooled engines will have one or more sacrificial zinc anodes screwed into their blocks somewhere. Many indirectly cooled engines also have anodes in their various heat exchangers.

The anode's role is to reduce the electrolytic corrosion that occurs when metals are in contact with an electrolyte—in this case, seawater. The zinc wastes away so that more important components will survive. Unfortunately, they waste away unseen, with no external sign that they have become depleted (Figure 12.15).

The engine manual will tell you how many anodes there are and how often they must be changed—every year is typical. The manual will also tell you where they are located, which is helpful since they aren't exactly conspicuous. Replacing an anode is simply a matter of unscrewing it and popping in a new one.

CARE OF AIR FILTERS

It's all too easy to neglect air filters. The relatively dust-free environments in which we keep our boats tend to make us unconcerned. And yet the gradual build-up of particles does happen—an insidious process that gradually chokes off the air and robs our engines of power.

Maintenance will depend on what type of air filter you have (Figure 12.16). The alternatives are:

- Paper element. These can't be rejuvenated. Simply throw away the old one when it becomes clogged and replace it with a new one.
- Synthetic wadding, usually trapped in a metal or plastic cage. This can be washed in a water and detergent solution. Allow to dry before refitting.
- Oil bath type. Very much yesterday's technology. A screen made up of coarse strands of metal is positioned over a shallow reservoir of oil, which mists upward to leave a sticky deposit on the screen. The reservoir should be emptied and cleaned periodically. Flush the screen out in diesel fuel or kerosene to remove particles stuck to it.

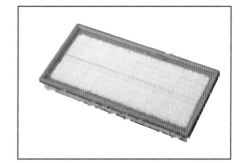

Figure 12.16   A typical paper element air filter.

CHAPTER

13

Emergency Procedures

DEPENDABLE THOUGH THEY USUALLY ARE, diesel engines aren't above throwing the occasional tantrum. In earlier chapters we have touched on preventive measures and tips to get you home, but that still leaves you potentially prey to sudden events that, at best, are merely inconvenient and occasionally may be downright dangerous. In those circumstances it's helpful to know what to do.

ENGINE OVERHEATS BECAUSE OF THERMOSTAT FAILURE

If the overheat alarm sounds when there's a good flow of water from the exhaust, stop the engine immediately. First check for a broken or slack drive belt. If you can eliminate this as the problem, the next most likely culprit is the thermostat, which will probably have failed in the closed position (Figure 13.1).

1. Do nothing until the engine has cooled. Remember, the freshwater coolant will be boiling hot and under pressure. Don't release the pressure cap until you're absolutely certain it's safe to do so.

(a)

(b)

Figure 13.1 When thermostat failure causes engine to overheat, cut the supports and remove the thermostat's innards (a), then replace the carcass so it will partially restrict the flow (b).

2. Remove the top of the thermostat housing and lift out the thermostat. On some engines you can reestablish the waterflow by simply discarding the valve and reassembling the housing. But a better move is to yank out the valve's moving parts so you're left with its empty carcass.

3. Then put everything back together as if normal and top up the coolant level. Although, of course, the thermostat won't be working at all, what remains of it will partially restrict the coolant flow to something like its usual rate. The engine will run a little cooler than is ideal, but at least you can restart it and continue on your way.

BYPASSING THE IGNITION SWITCH OR SOLENOID

Key-type switches are notoriously temperamental. If you turn the key and nothing at all happens—i.e., no clicks from the starter motor or solenoid—first check that the isolation switch is on and that the battery isn't flat. Then bypass the switch at the starter solenoid by bridging across the terminals used by the two smaller wires as shown (Figure 13.2).

If this is unsuccessful, the solenoid is probably faulty, in which case you can try the following:

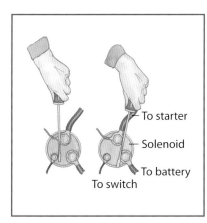

Figure 13.2 Bypassing the ignition switch (left) or solenoid (right).

- There will be a pair of heavy terminals on the end of the solenoid—the power feed to the starter motor itself. The object is to connect them together with a screwdriver blade as shown. A lot of current will be conducted, so expect some spectacular arcing. And be careful not to touch the surrounding metalwork with the screwdriver, since this will produce a dead short circuit.
- If the starter motor is of the inertia type, this is all you need to do for it to operate. On pre-engaged motors, however, the solenoid serves a dual function: it engages the pinion with the flywheel and also closes the main switch points to allow current to flow to the motor. If the latter is the problem you might get yourself out of trouble by having someone hold the starter switch in the "ON" position while you bridge across the terminals.

STOPPING A "RUNAWAY" ENGINE

Most of us will never encounter this problem—and just as well—since it can provide unwelcome levels of excitement. The term describes an engine that continues to run after the fuel supply has been shut off. The usual causes could include a fault in the internal throttle mechanism or lubrication oil being sucked into the cylinders from an overfilled crankcase or past worn piston rings, or even failed turbocharger oil seals. Not only will the engine refuse to stop, it may also rev out of control—even to the point where it disintegrates! You wouldn't want to be anywhere near when that happens.

- First shut off the fuel. This won't stop the engine, but at least it isolates the problem. Put the engine under load if possible—even straining against its mooring lines. This may keep the situation under control until its unconventional supply of fuel is exhausted.
- Since diesels only need fuel and air to run, and the runaway is drawing on its own source of fuel, the only commodity you can control is the air supply. Try blocking the air intake with a thick book, a heavy cushion, or even a noninflatable life jacket. Keep your fingers well away from that suction, which will be prodigious!
- A Halon (now banned) or CO_2 fire extinguisher discharged into the air intake will have the same effect.
- If all else fails, vacate the boat or, if at sea, get as far away from the engine as possible.

DEALING WITH AN ENGINE FIRE

Fire on a boat is a truly terrifying event—potentially deadly if that boat is at sea. Fortunately, diesel engines, with their simple electrics and high flash-point fuel, are relatively safe in this regard. But that doesn't mean they are immune.

Many engine spaces are protected by automatic heat-triggered extinguishers that discharge at a pre-set temperature—68°C (154°F) and 79°C (174°F) being typical, depending on the type. Some of these systems can also be actuated manually by remote control. Other engine spaces have a small extinguisher port that can be opened to allow a portable extinguisher to be discharged through it (Figure 13.3). The ideal arrangement is to have both.

Figure 13.3   An engine box extinguisher port is a good alternative or addition to an automatic system.

1. Stop the engine if it is still running. Shut off the fuel and electrics.
2. Do not open up the engine space. A smoldering fire can become an inferno if invigorated by oxygen. Starved of air, a fire will dwindle and die.
3. Try to discharge an extinguisher into the engine space. More than one, if possible. The quantity of the extinguishing agent is everything—in other words, a 2 kg (4.4 lb.) extinguisher will be twice as effective as a 1 kg (2.2 lb.) one. If there isn't a dedicated extinguisher port, there may be a vent in the engine box, or even a hole somewhere that will serve.
4. While one crew member fights the fire, others should be preparing to abandon ship if necessary. Fire spreads quickly when out of control—and it's not just the flames you should worry about. Older foam cushions give off hydrogen cyanide when burning. Just a single lungful can kill.

Index

Numbers in **bold** indicate pages with illustrations